ALAN McCREDIE has been a professional photographer and filmmaker for over ten years, working with most of the major agencies in Scotland and beyond. Working in all fields of photography he is best known for his documentary work and has completed several major projects in this area to critical acclaim. He is a Perthshire man lost to Leith.

Edinburgh the Dreich

a celebration of all that is dreich

ALAN McCREDIE

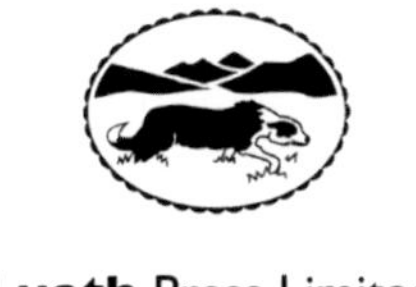

Luath Press Limited

EDINBURGH

www.luath.co.uk

First published 2021
Reprinted 2023

ISBN: 978-1-910022-82-5

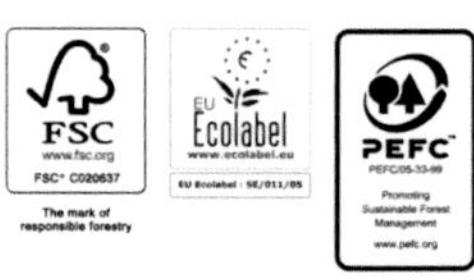

Printed and bound by Robertson Printers, Forfar

Typeset in 11 point Avenir Next
by Main Point Books, Edinburgh

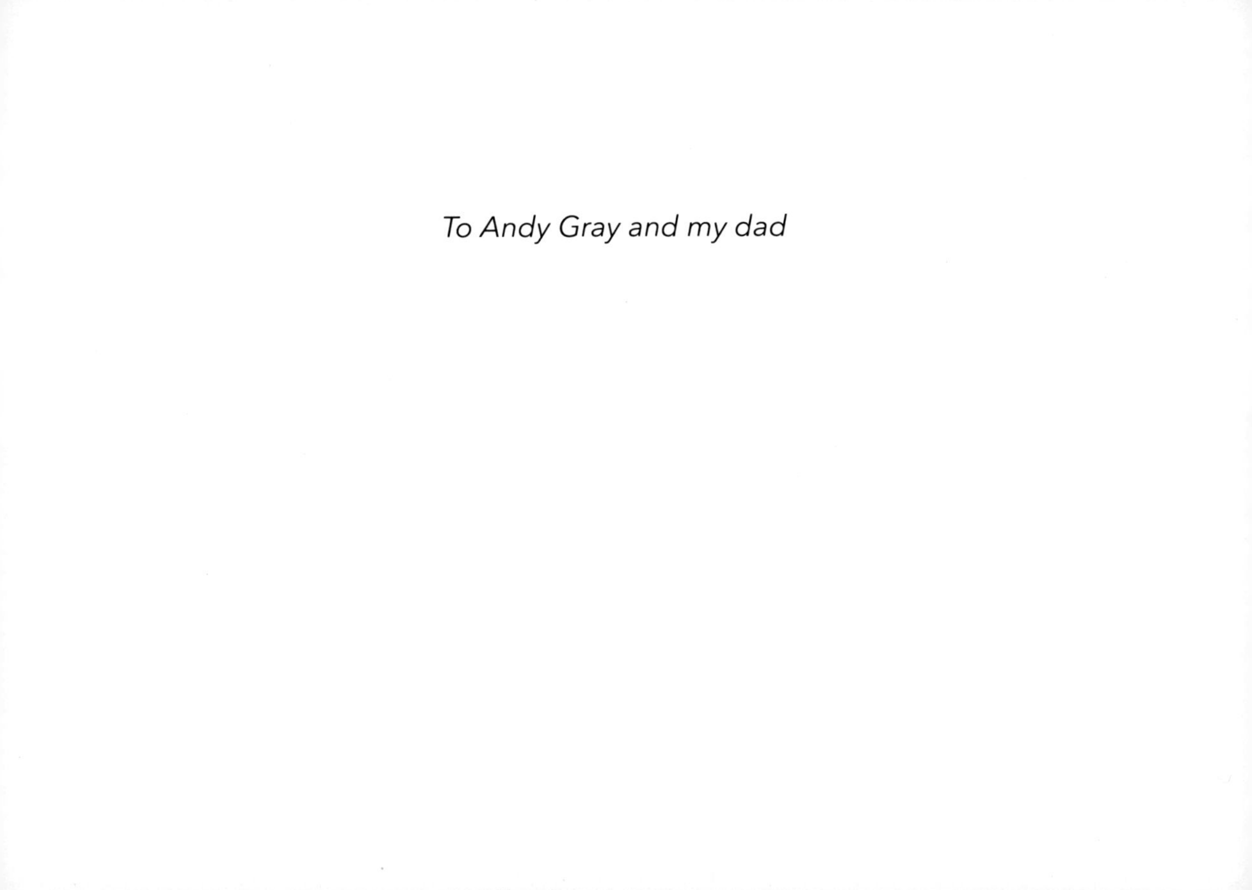

To Andy Gray and my dad

dreich

/driːx/

adjective SCOTTISH

(especially of weather) dreary; bleak.
"a cold, dreich early April day"

Has there ever been a time in most of our lifetimes, at least in the west, that has been more dreich than the last 18 months? A genuinely miserable period that has seen the world stagger from one wave of COVID-19 to another, with even now, no real clear sign of an end on the horizon. To embark on a book celebrating the more dismal side of life may have seemed foolish, but when we are surrounded by darkness even the merest hint of gloom can seem like a supernova has just bloomed into existence.

Dreich, as many of you know, can be used to describe more than just a type of wet, dismal, dark and dreary day. It is in this context that it is most widely used, but like all good words, its meaning can change over time, and it can happily been used to describe a whole plethora of occasions. The origins of the word are Germanic and correspond to the Old Norse word *drjugr* meaning enduring, lasting, long-suffering. This became the Old English *dree* or *dreigh* and the step to dreich was simple. In the *Dictionary of the Scots Language* the meteorological definition of dreich comes far down the list behind older meanings such as weariness, monotonous, tediousness, tardy, lacking inspiration and rather worryingly, slow to pay debts. These definitions have now essentially fallen out of use but were handy in choosing some of the photographs for the book as I was keen to avoid 50 photos of overcast days. These different definitions gave me more scope to experiment with different subjects. I wanted to look at the idea of dreich as a state of mind as well as a state of weather and there is plenty of scope for this approach in Scotland, or any other country. Therefore, I allowed myself some leeway in how I approached the photography for the book, which I hope has given a more varied and interesting appeal.

One very important point that I simply cannot stress enough is that I believe all of the subjects photographed in this book have a real beauty to them. To me, 'dreich' has become a positive word. Some of the photos you will see may conventionally be described as 'dreich', but to me they are lovely. I decided from the very beginning that I needed to be careful when choosing some of the images in order not to cause offence (even though none would ever have been intended) – I rejected some photos that showed rows of houses as these were happily inhabited, and although to me I thought they looked wonderful, it just doesn't seem right to describe other people's homes as dreich, however much I may think the word has a positive meaning.

I have been, admittedly, stretching the definition of dreich to accommodate some of the images in this book. For instance there is a photograph of a brutalist Edinburgh building, taken on a warm, sunny day. Not meterologically dreich at all, and as a lover of brutalist buildings not remotely dreich architecturally either in my opinion. Photos like this have been included because often the general concensus applies a certain level of dreichness to the subjects of these images – one I almost entirely disagree with. The conventional wisdom may define some of these photographs as unattractive, unloved or of course dreich, but in every case my heart would leap at the sight of them. Beauty in ugliness may be harder to find, but is infinitely more rewarding when it is.

As I mentioned earlier, all of this was set against, and photographed during the COVID-19 pandemic. If ever there was a time to find joy in the mundane, happiness in the dismal, beauty in the forgotten places, this was and is that time. The small, simple pleasures of life have never seemed so important than they have done in the last year and a half.

The pandemic also had another more physical effect on the book – much of the photography was done during 2020 when travel restrictions were somewhat tighter than they are now and this translated directly in the locations of the photographs I took. At one point you would be about to start looking at a book that contained 50 dreich images of my street (something that was worryingly easy to do). Thankfully things have eased somewhat so I did manage to get out of my immediate environs although one or two of those early images have survived through to the final cut.

I decided early on not to be a slave to the weather, and as I have already mentioned, dreichness is more much more than just a wet, grey day. And yet, every time the classic dreich day presented itself, I would get twitchy, knowing that for all my protestations of other meanings for the word, the classic dreich day still just makes for a great backdrop to a photograph. So try as I might, a large amount of dampness definitely seeps into the images.

This book is most definitely a celebration of all that is dreich. The images here would not adorn any tartan-edged shortbread tin, but I would hope they are all the more interesting because of that. There is of course always a place for conventional beauty in photography but there must also always be a place for the opposite of that. Dreich to me is the melancholy, not the miserable, the overlooked, not the obvious. Would a sunny day in Scotland be quite as exquisite without the knowledge that we had to endure 9 million rainy days to achieve it? If I have learnt anything from the last 18 months it is that having the ability to find joy in almost anything is the real key to happiness.

Enjoy the dreich, it is your dreariest friend!

Alan McCredie
Edinburgh
October 2021

Acknowledgements

Thanks are due to my wife, Jenny, who is always a great support and even better picture editor. A special thanks to The Rig Fish Bar for allowing me to 'borrow' some chips to photograph (I ate them) and to the weather, which in Scotland is always on my side.
I am eternally grateful to all the staff at Luath, who do the real work.

They Don't Make 'Em Like They Used To

Once Annette would style the ladies, and Jim would groom the men,
and a short step would take you to Ibiza where you could develop
that beating Balearic tan.

All gone now though, just an old dream on a cold day.

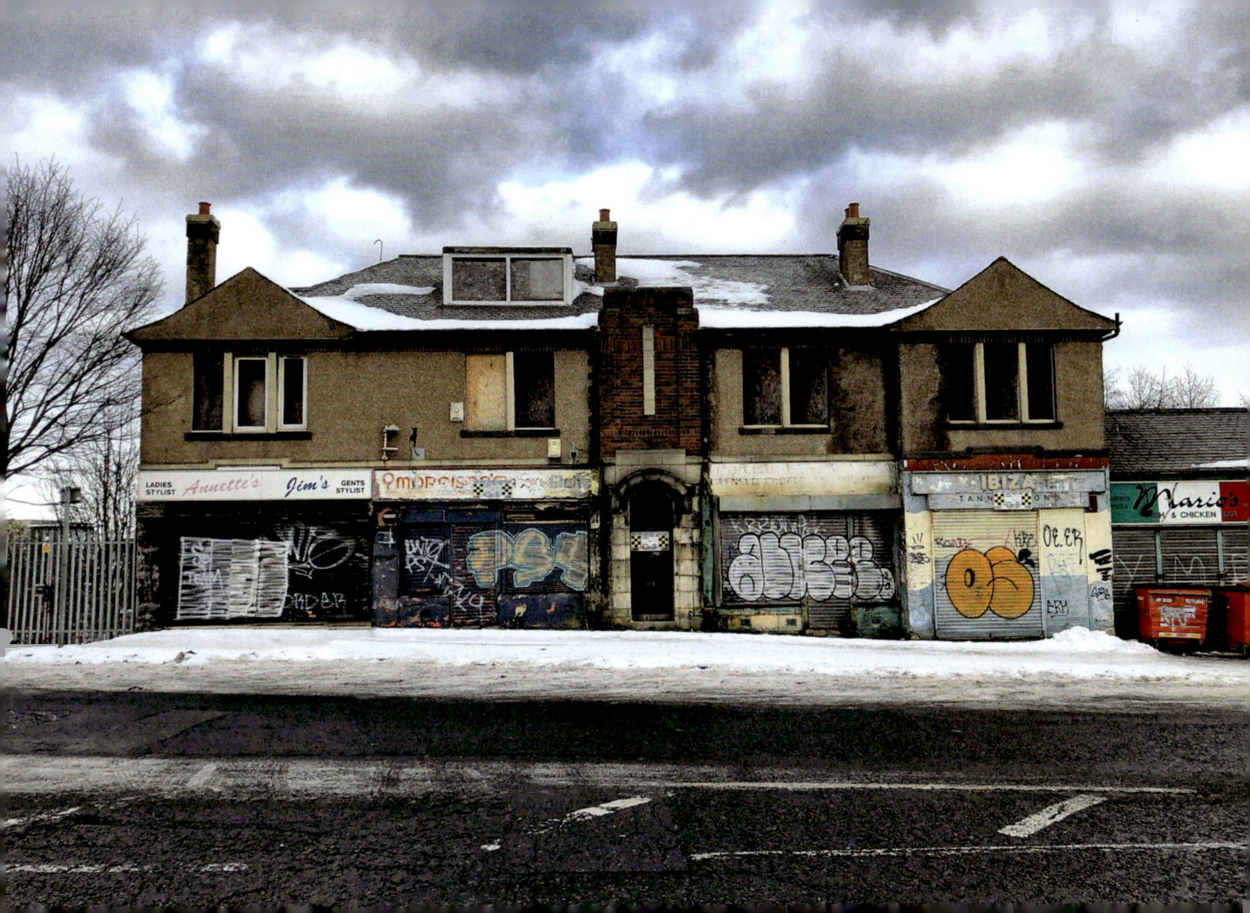

LADIES STYLIST
Annette's
Jim's
GENTS STYLIST
Morrisons
IBIZA
TANNING
Mario's
& CHICKEN BAR

Strength Through Power Or Power Through Strength?

It all seemed to start with Olga Korbut and Nadia Comăneci in those jittery TV days of the 1972 and 1976 Olympic Games. Now the 'perfect ten' is achievable throughout the parks of Edinburgh.

6 out of 10 for this effort though...

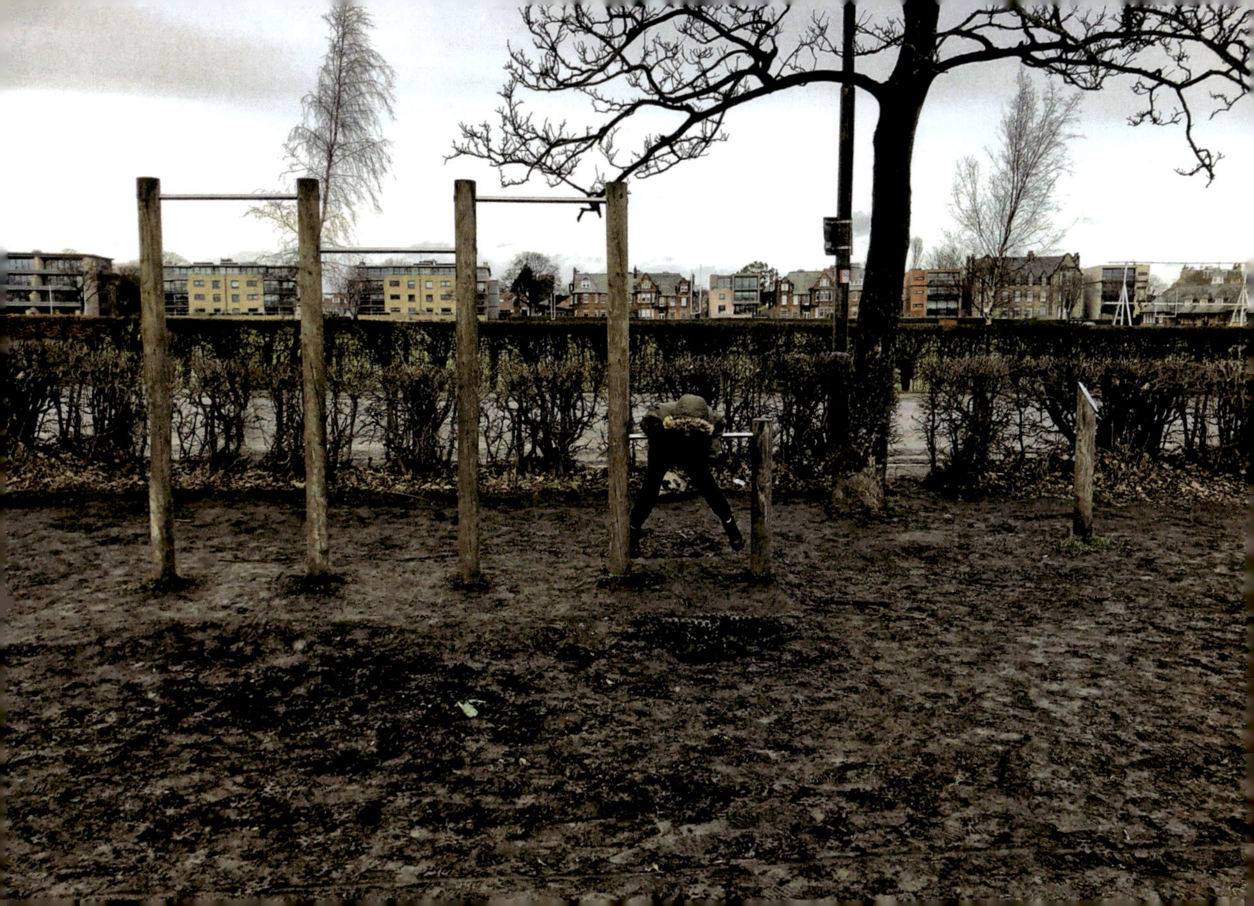

Life Without Buildings

The most evocative of all the old shop fronts of Edinburgh is sadly no more, as the creeping gentrification of parts of the city continue to devour the character it once had.

Sleep well Beldam Lascar, the evil genius of a thousand unwritten adventure novels.

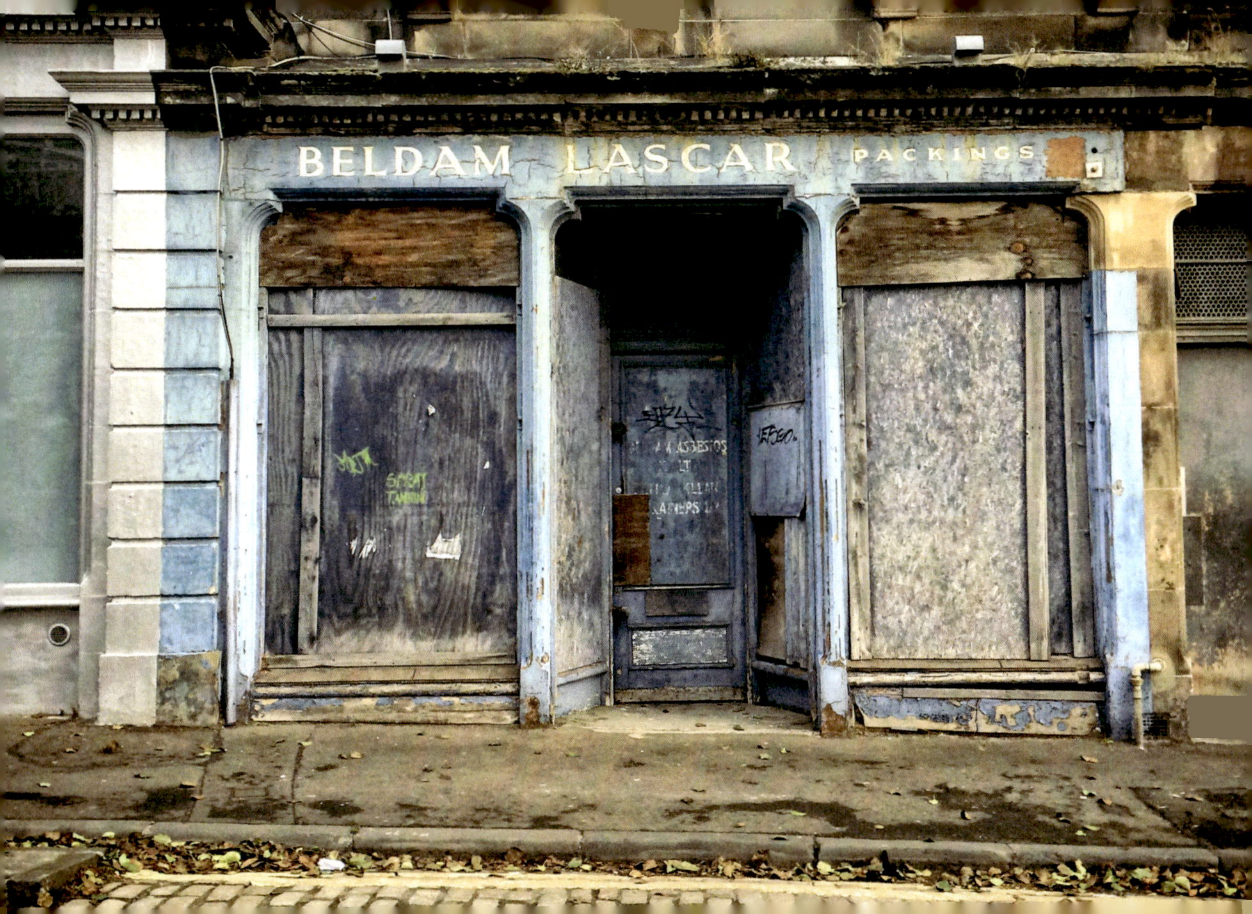

BELDAM LASCAR PACKINGS

Red and Green Should Never Be Seen

Which came first – the postbox or the hedge? Like the twitter meme of Homer Simpson disappearing into a hedge, here we have the real life equivalent.

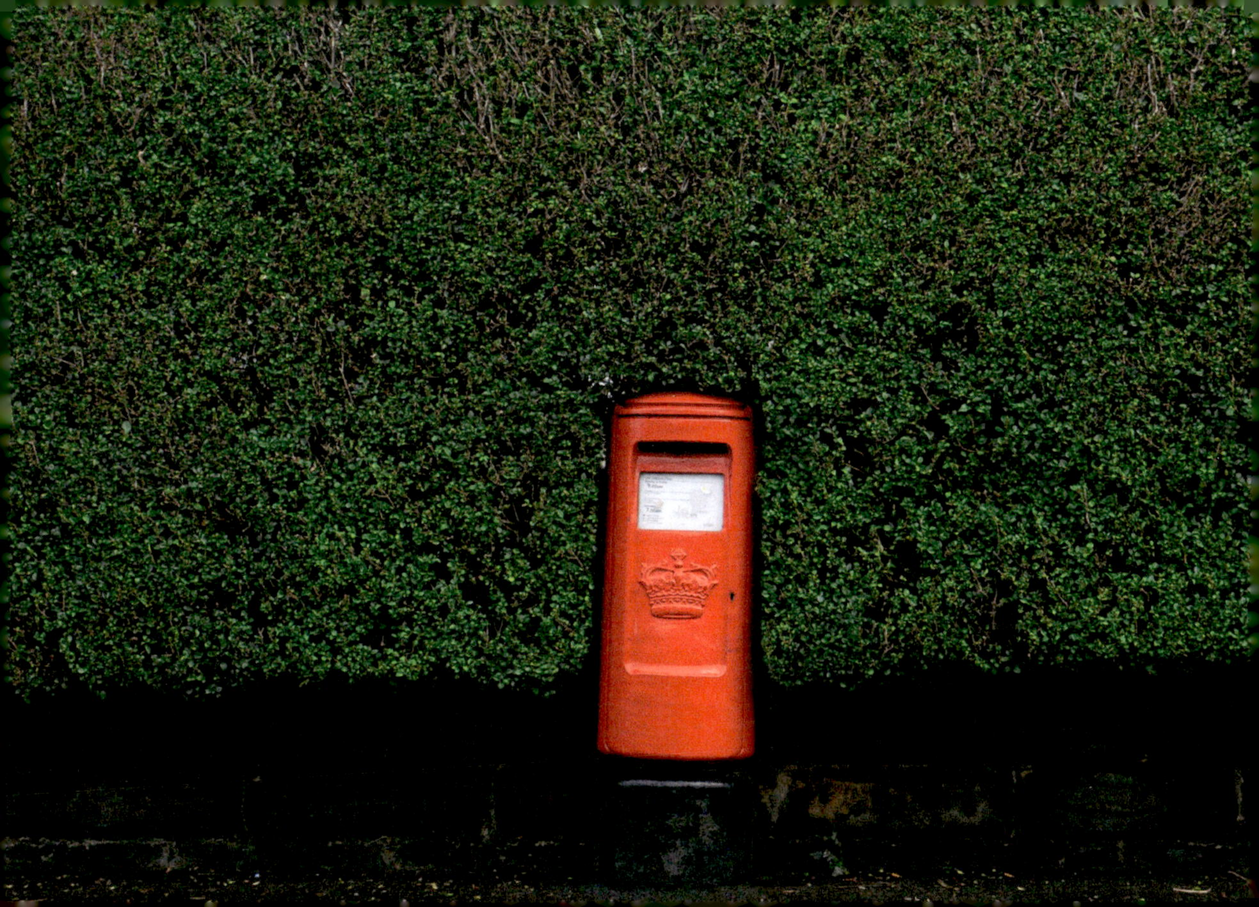

The Cold Moons

Silhouetted by a winter moon, the trees form an orderly queue.
Waiting with infinite patience for the coming of spring and the
re-awakening of the world.

Winging It

With global warming a clear and present danger, every avenue and dual-carriageway is being explored for solutions. One answer may be to cut your car in two and instantly reduce emissions by 50 per cent.

Drastic measures for drastic times.

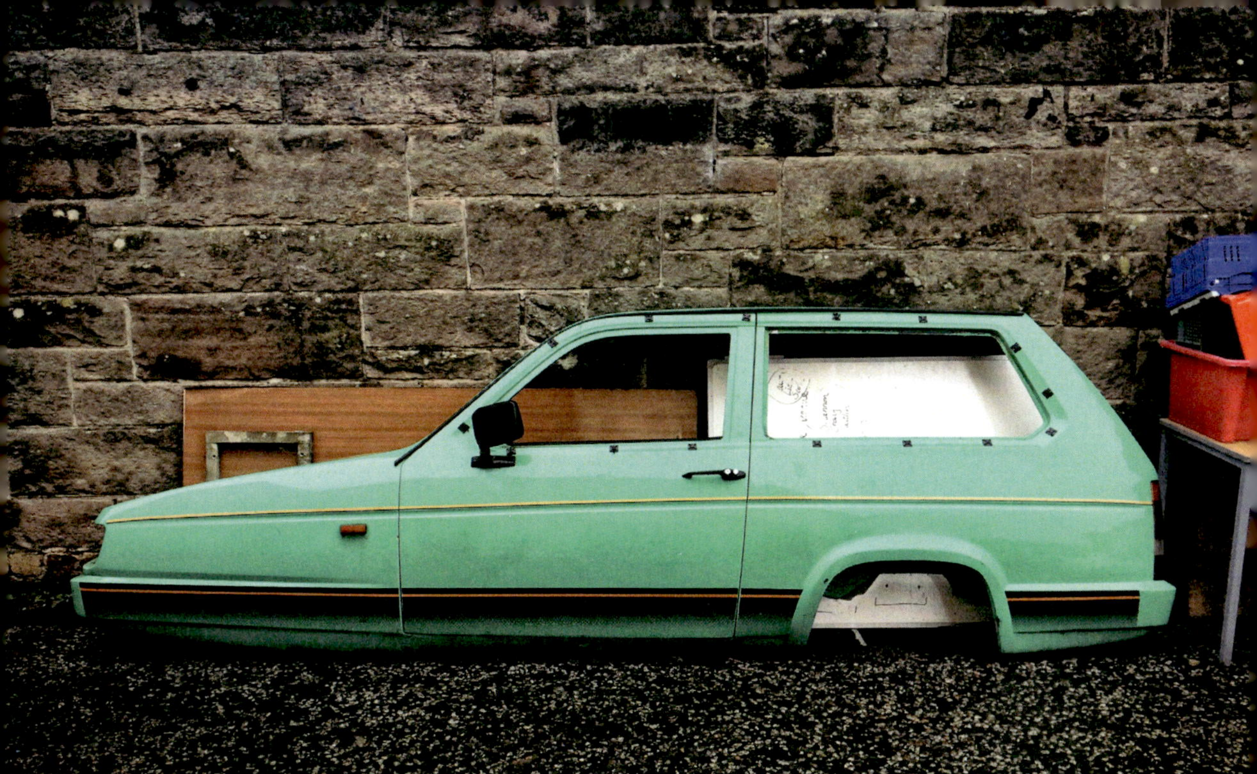

The Desire Paths Of Our Youth

Festival accomodation in Edinburgh is getting harder to find.
This bijou property, featuring original period features and ample
parking is a snip at £4,000 pw.

No dogs please.

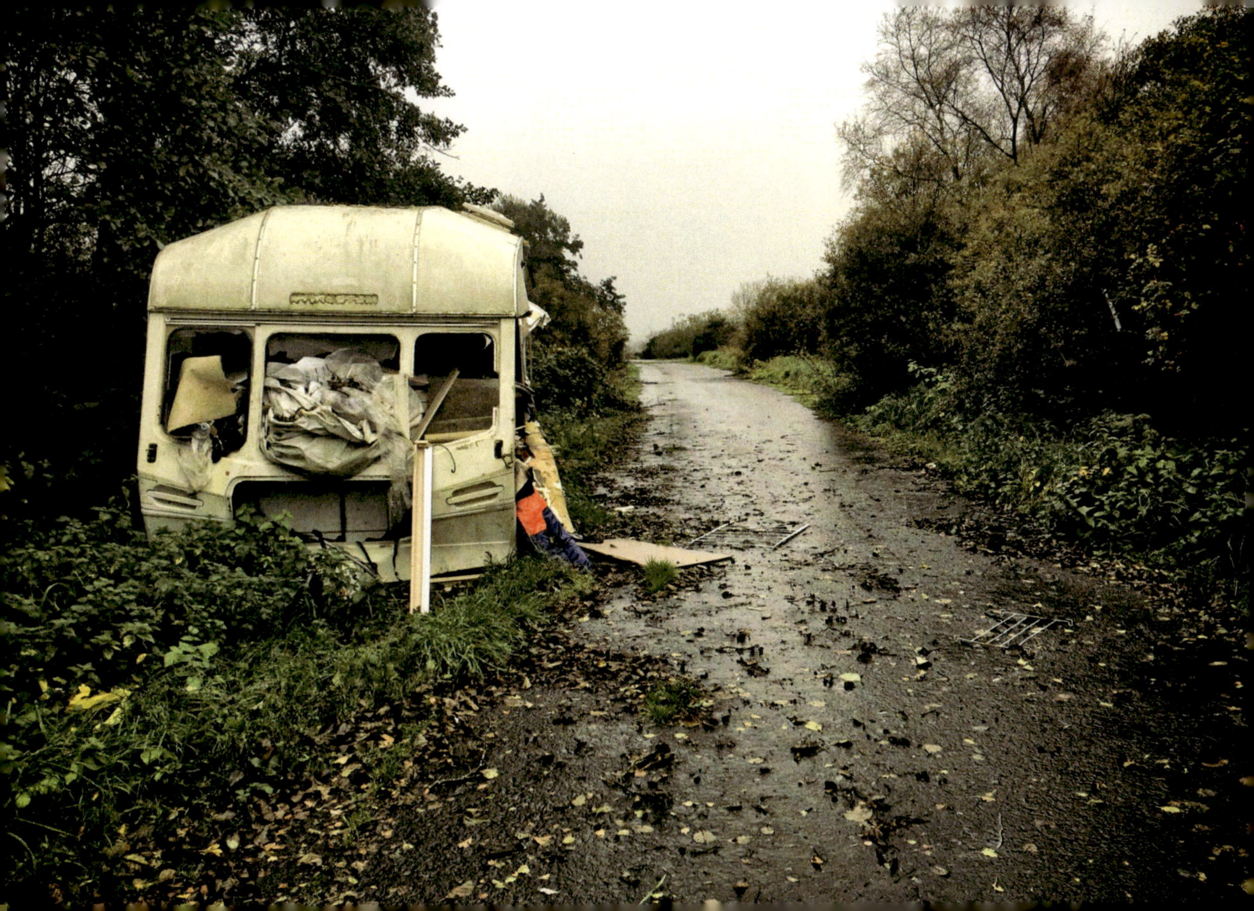

Letters From Other Lands

By 2050 there will be more shipping containers than there are people.
This is patently false but, my word, doesn't it seem like it is true?
They are the horse and cart, the cup and ring, the dolmen and menhir
of our age.

In the far future what strange spiritual significance will be endowed
upon them by the bewildered archaeologists of the age?

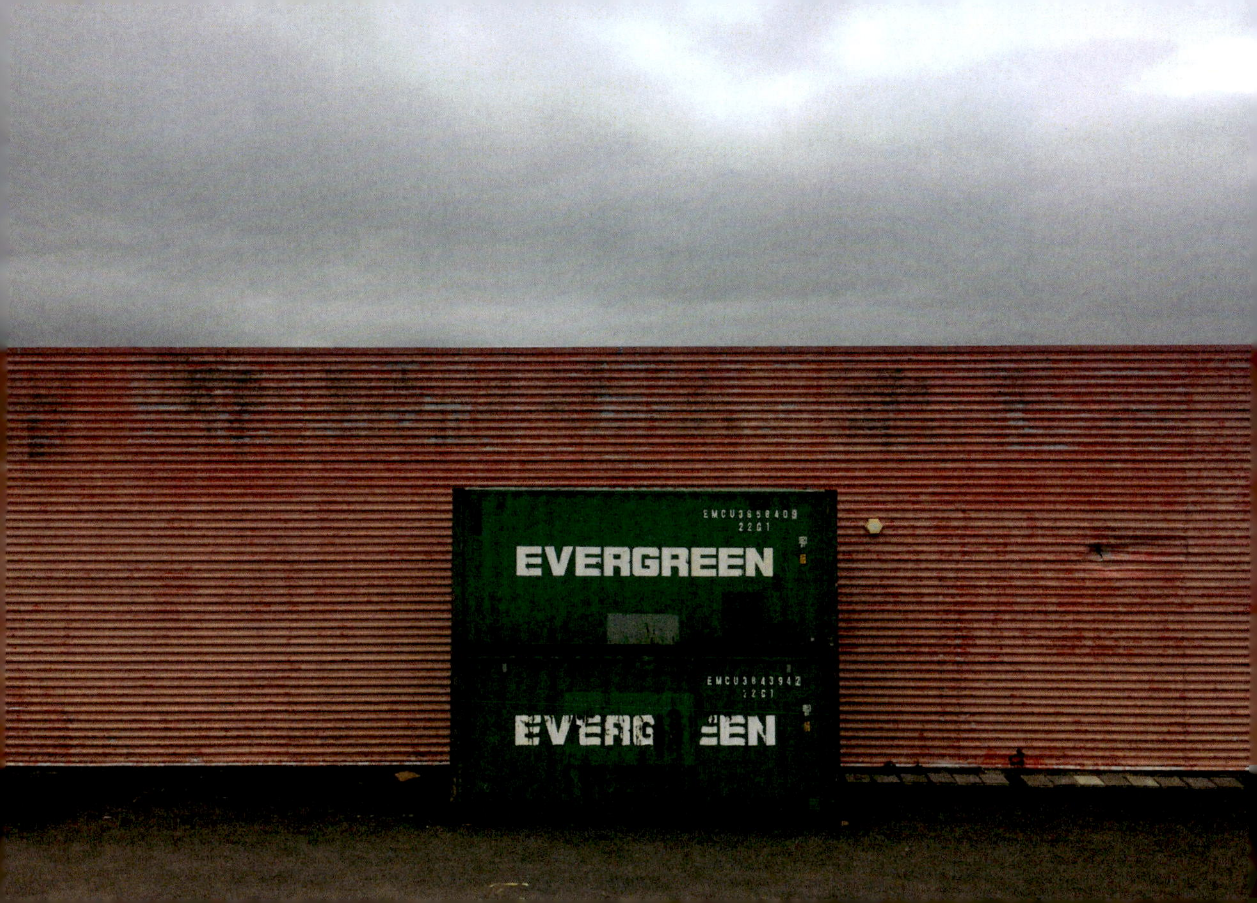
EMCU3658409
22G1
EVERGREEN
EMCU3843942
22G1
EVERG EEN

Imaginary Cities Of The North

Under certain weather conditions (ie dreich ones), Edinburgh is a city
that looks as if it is nothing more than a giant rock formation formed
aeons ago by unimaginable forces, hewn roughly out of the bedrock,
and strewn with the moraine of ancient glaciers. Yet when the sun comes
out it sparkles like a diamond placed before a star.

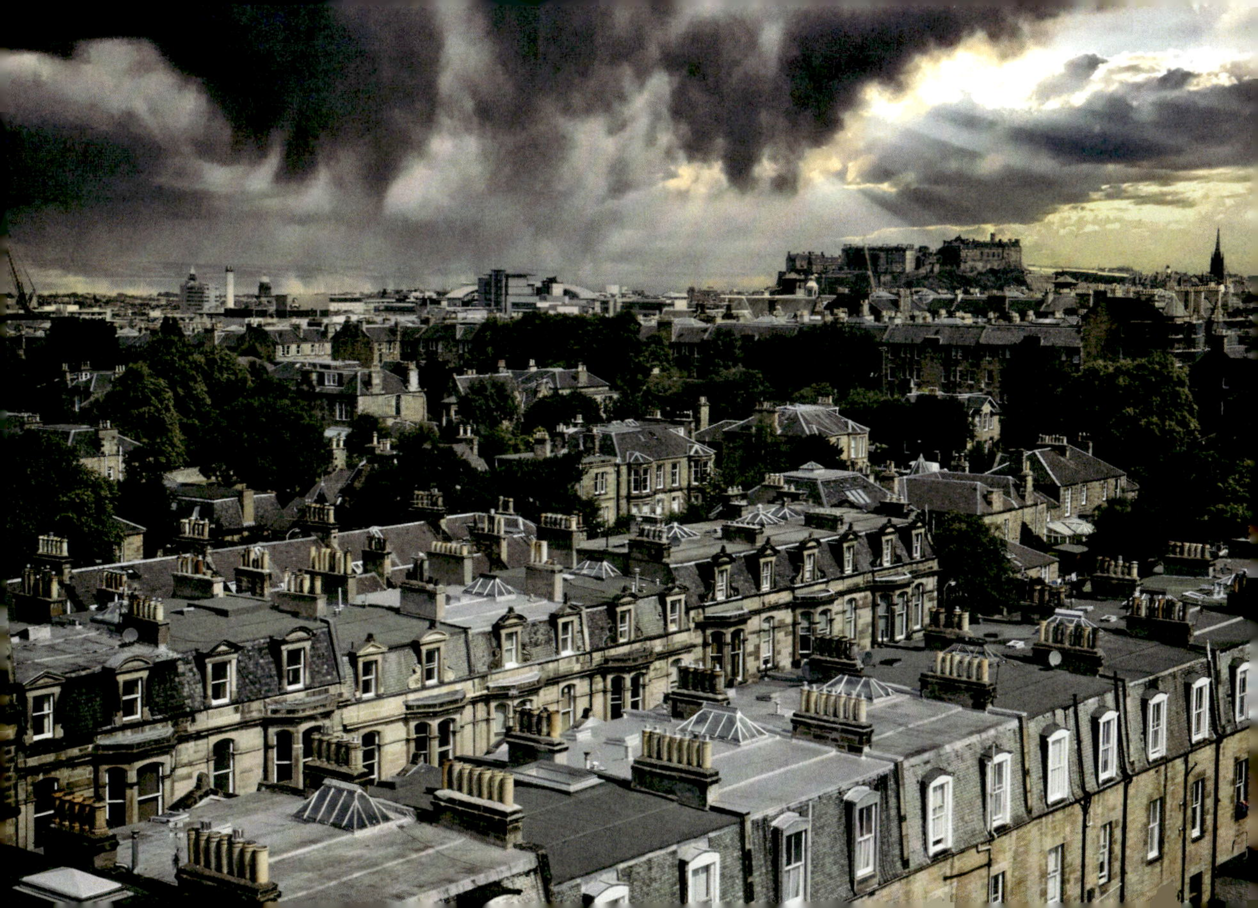

Understanding Is A Curious Point Of View

It can be hard in our modern world to keep up with changes in trends, or new conventions in naming, or even working out how to pay for a quick trip on the Edinburgh tram.

Thankfully some of the old ways remain and if you need some stuff to clean your windows, you can find it here. A lighthouse of simplicity in the midst of a confusing world (and make no mistake, the glass in that lighthouse is SPOTLESS).

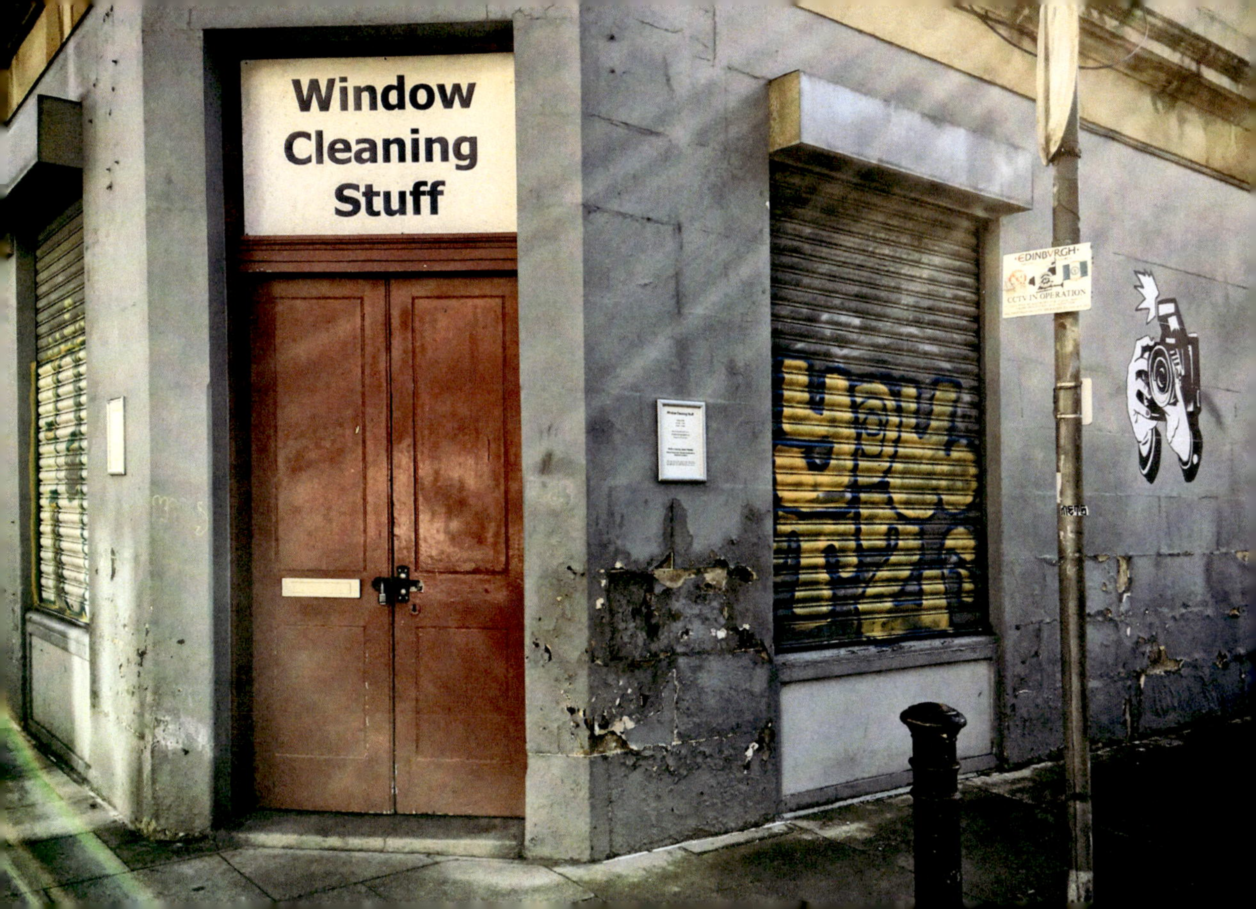
Window
Cleaning
Stuff
EDINBVRGH
CCTV IN OPERATION

Laughing In The Darkness

Built in 1950, the Western Harbour Breakwater Lighthouse is one of the most obvious abandoned buildings in the city. There is something maagical about lighthouses and it is always a great sadness to see them decommissioned and decaying. Time moves on, but a light in the darkness is always needed.

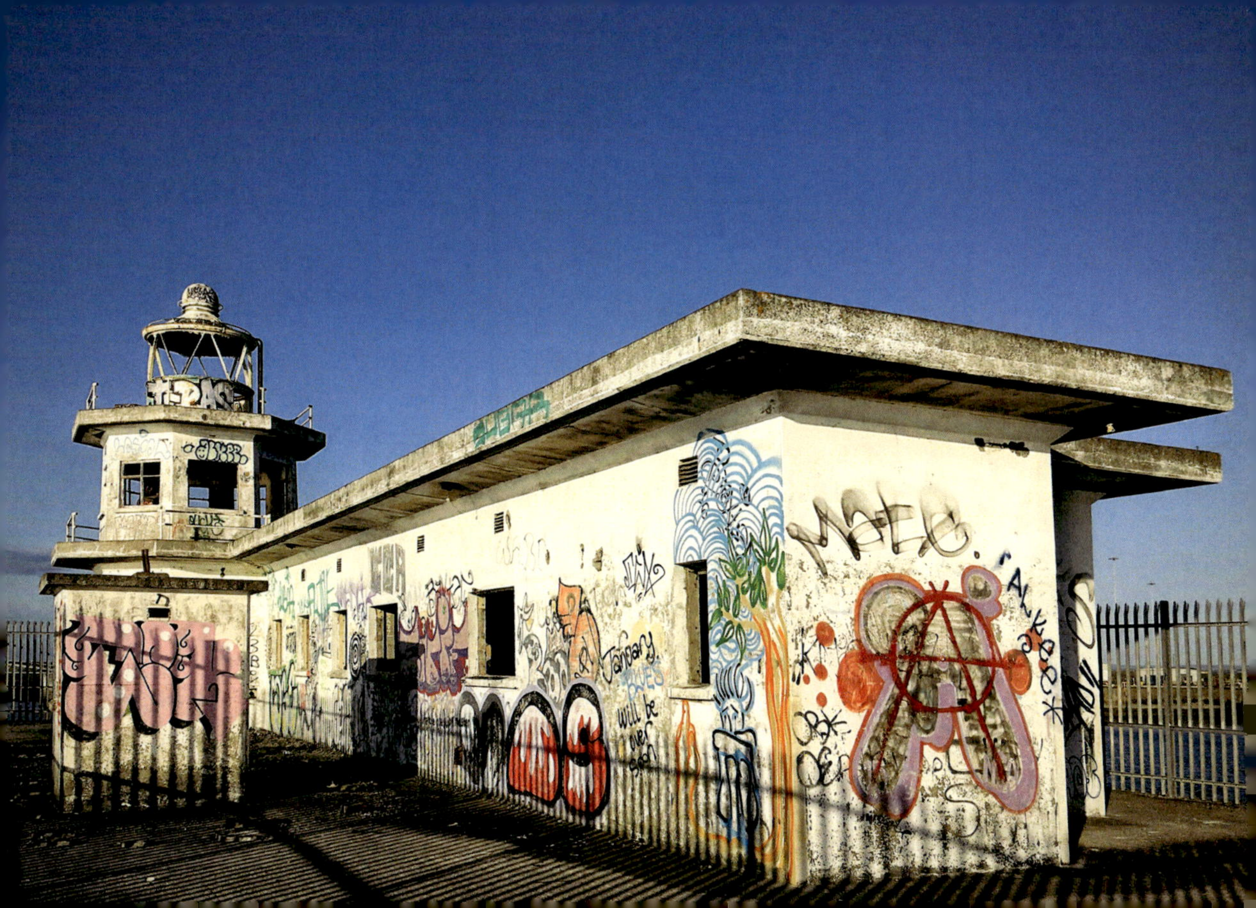

The Ocean Fell To Its Knees

In a city it can be hard to see the approaching weather. Thankfully Edinburgh has the great basalt lump that is Arthur's Seat well within the city boundaries and from this vantage point, looking to the east, the oncoming rain clouds are clearly visible.

Can you make it down from the hill in time to avoid a soaking?

An Ocean Of Angels

Beneath a turbulent sky, whipped to distraction by an angry western gale, the swans of St Margaret's Loch brace, and turn their foreheads to windward.

Honk, honk against the dying of the light.

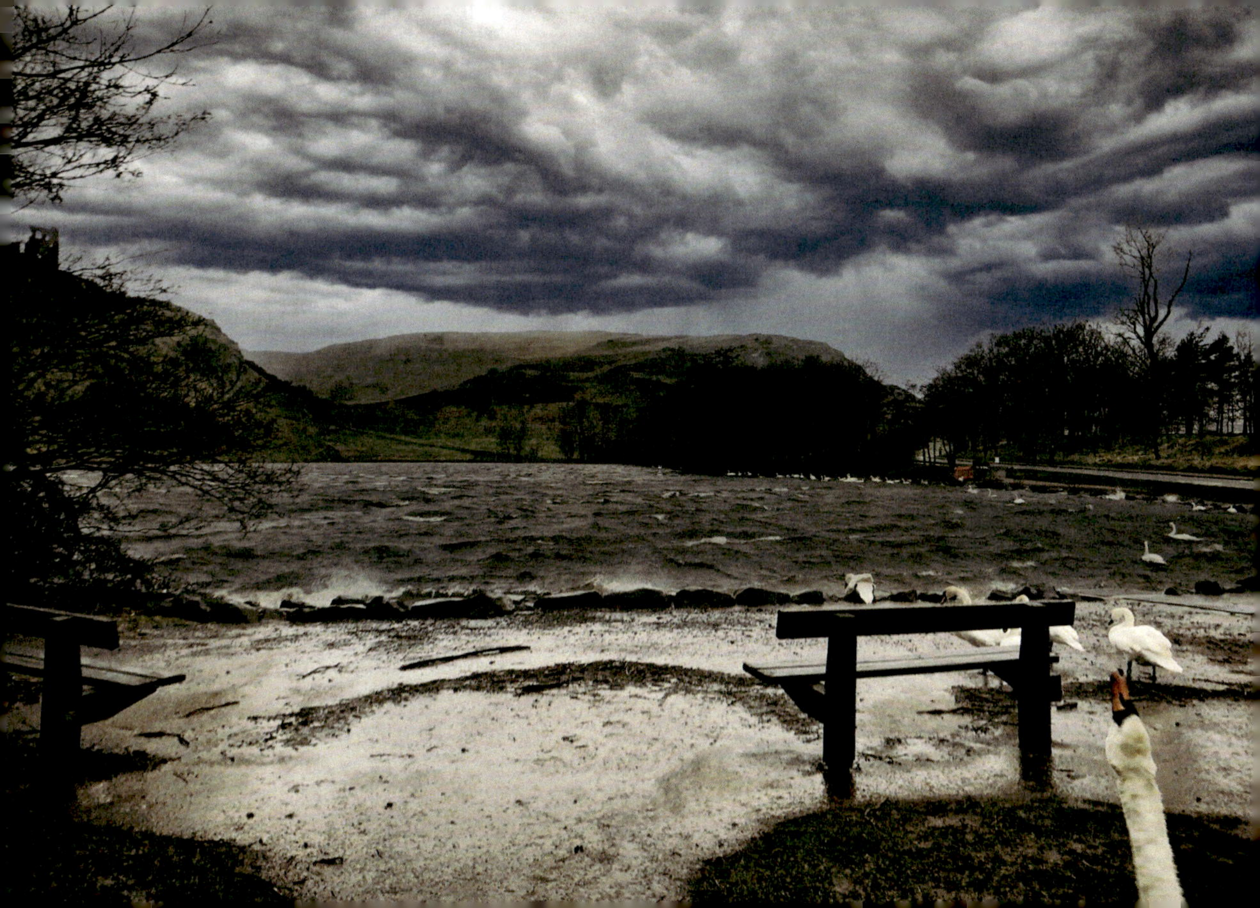

I Like Smoke And Lightning, Heavy Metal Thunder

On a cold winter's night sometime in early 1968, wide collars turned up against the damp, the pioneers of metal assembled here. And with an almighty drum roll were formed the gods of metal. Led Zeppelin, Deep Purple, Black Sabbath and Steppenwolf all originated right here in Metal Centre.

Alas the Metal Centre is no more, having been razed to the ground with one last crazed guitar riff in early 2021.

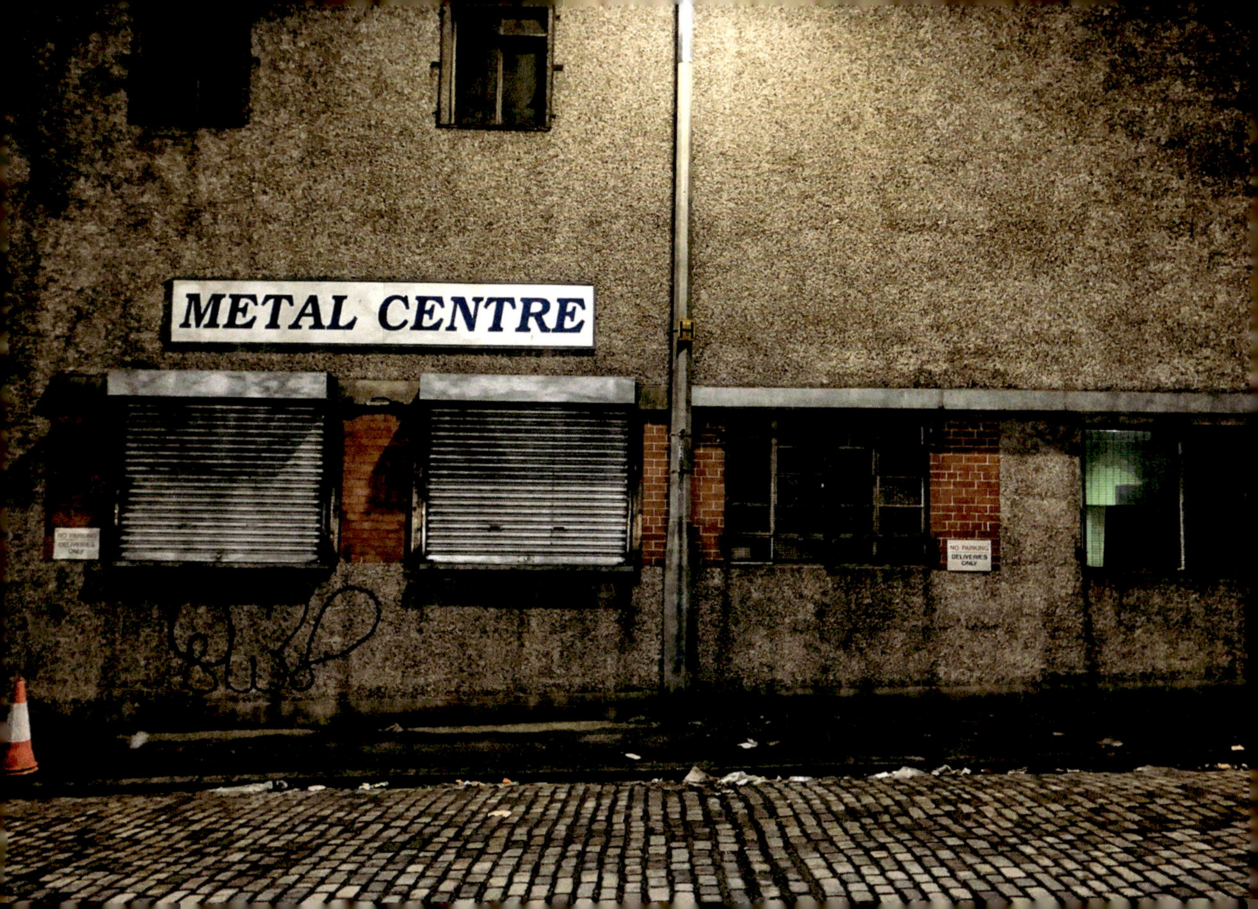
METAL CENTRE
NO PARKING
DELIVERIES
ONLY
NO PARKING
DELIVERIES
ONLY

Where Will This Tight-Lipped Dream Go?

Despite living in Edinburgh for decades, the abomination that is chips with salt and sauce is one I will never come to terms with. Unique to Edinburgh and the surrounding area the taste is hard to describe. It is essentially brown sauce cut with vinegar and laced with a liberal pinch of Deadly Nightshade. I have had to buy bottles of the stuff and take it to exiled Edinburghers, such is their passion for the brown acidic goo.

One deep whiff of the aroma is known to clear the airwaves for up to 48 hours.

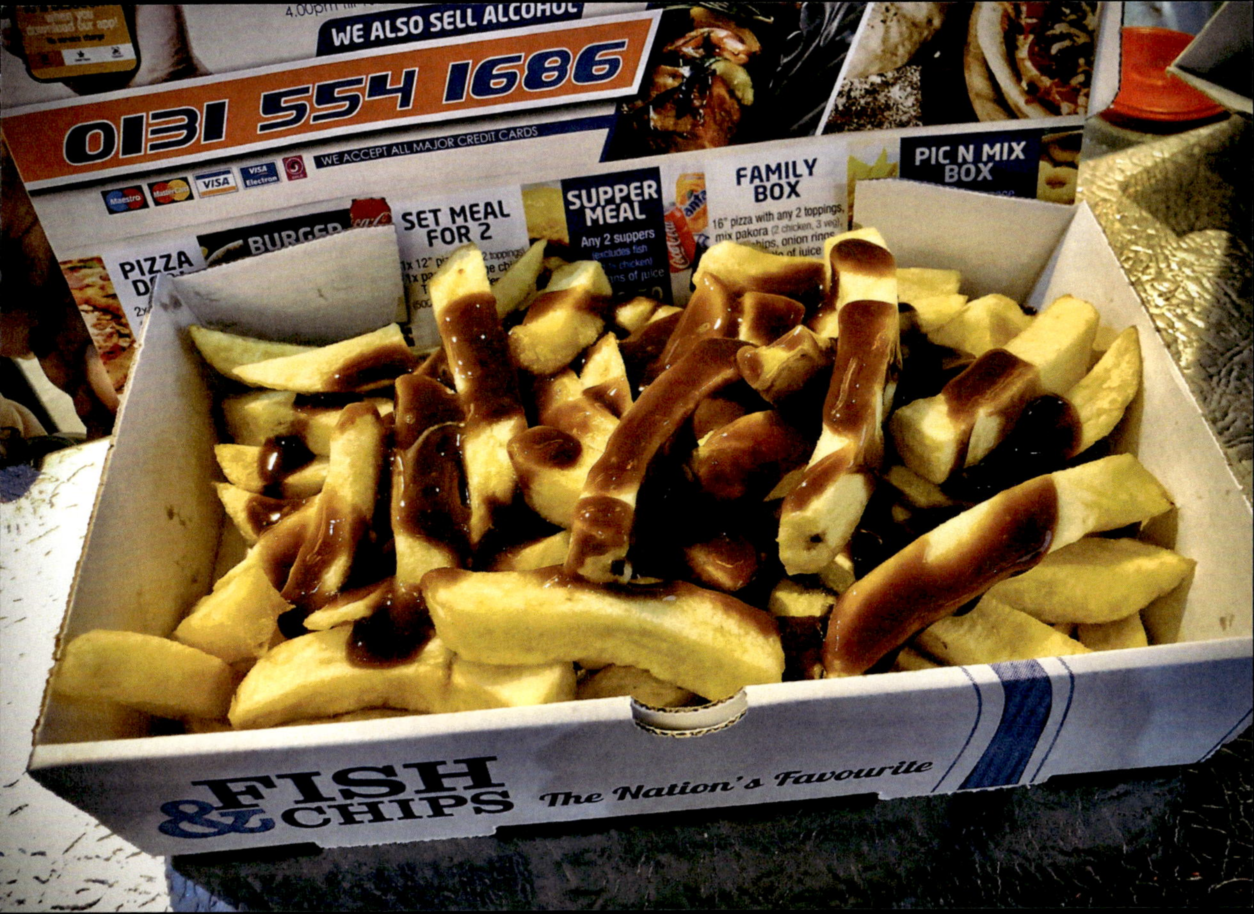

WE ALSO SELL ALCOHOL
0131 554 1686
WE ACCEPT ALL MAJOR CREDIT CARDS
Maestro
MasterCard
VISA
VISA Electron
PIZZA
BURGER
SET MEAL FOR 2
SUPPER MEAL
Any 2 suppers
FAMILY BOX
16" pizza with any 2 toppings, mix pakora (2 chicken, 3 veg), chips, onion rings
PIC N MIX BOX
FISH & CHIPS
The Nation's Favourite

Nights At The Circus

It happens in all cities. In the busy nightlife highlife city centre, flats can be bought cheaply. Once bought, the complaints against the noise that made them cheap in the first place intensify. In the property-developer heaven that is Edinburgh there can be only one winner.

The cultural void left behind creates whole areas that resemble a wet Sunday afternoon in 1972.

RIP Studio 24. We were in you for many many a wild night.

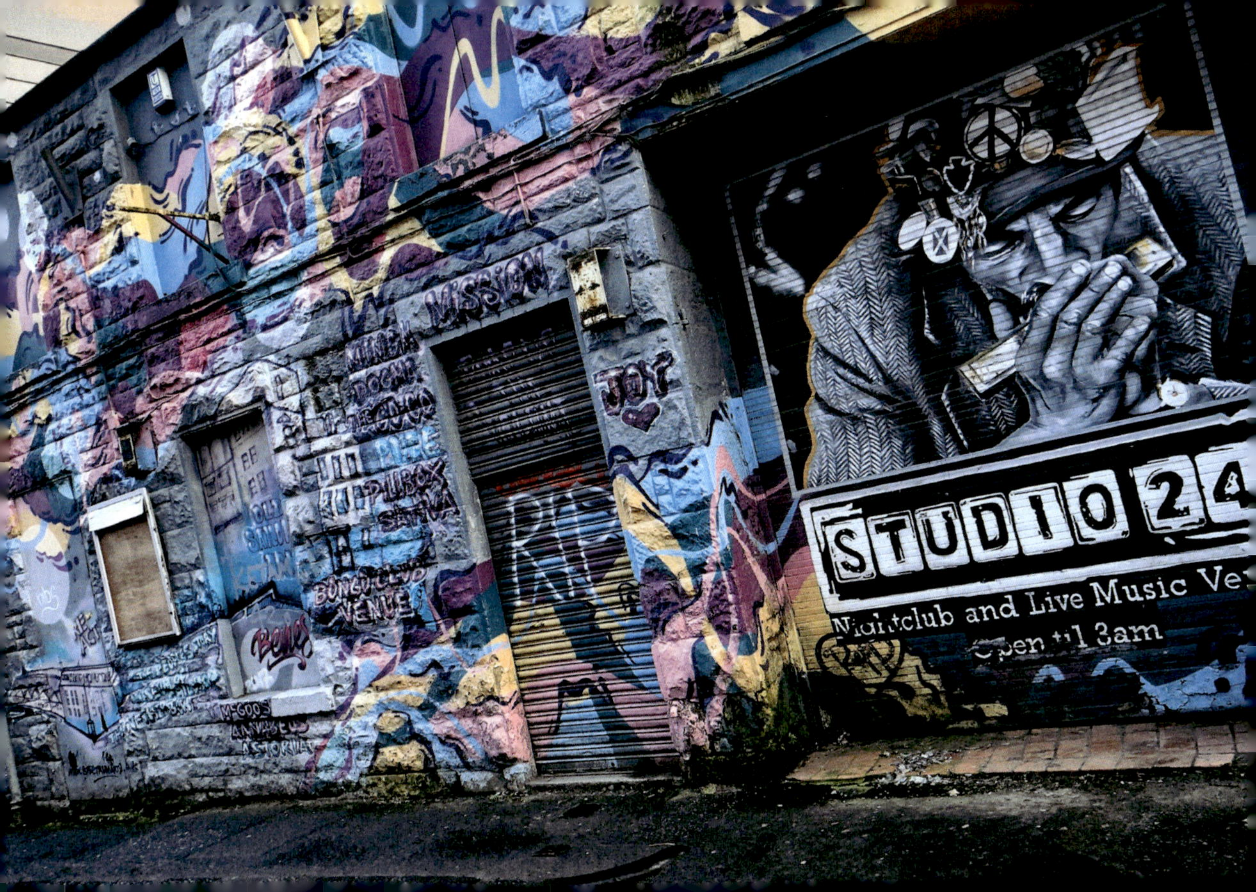

MISSION
JOY
STUDIO 24
Nightclub and Live Music Ve
Open til 3am
BONGO CLUB
VENUE

There Gloom The Dark, Broad Seas

A splash of colour against the murk. The wild flower growing amongst the rubble. Without the dark there would be no light so in the midst of a dismal world pandemic let us go down to the sea. And if there is no brightness there, we will bring our own with us.

A Painter Always Paints His Own Portrait

Those pesky kids!

Every time I see one of these burnt-out bikes my first thought is always 'I would have had that!'

As a point of interest this is the actual bike in Meat Loaf's bonkers rock anthem 'Bat Out Of Hell'.

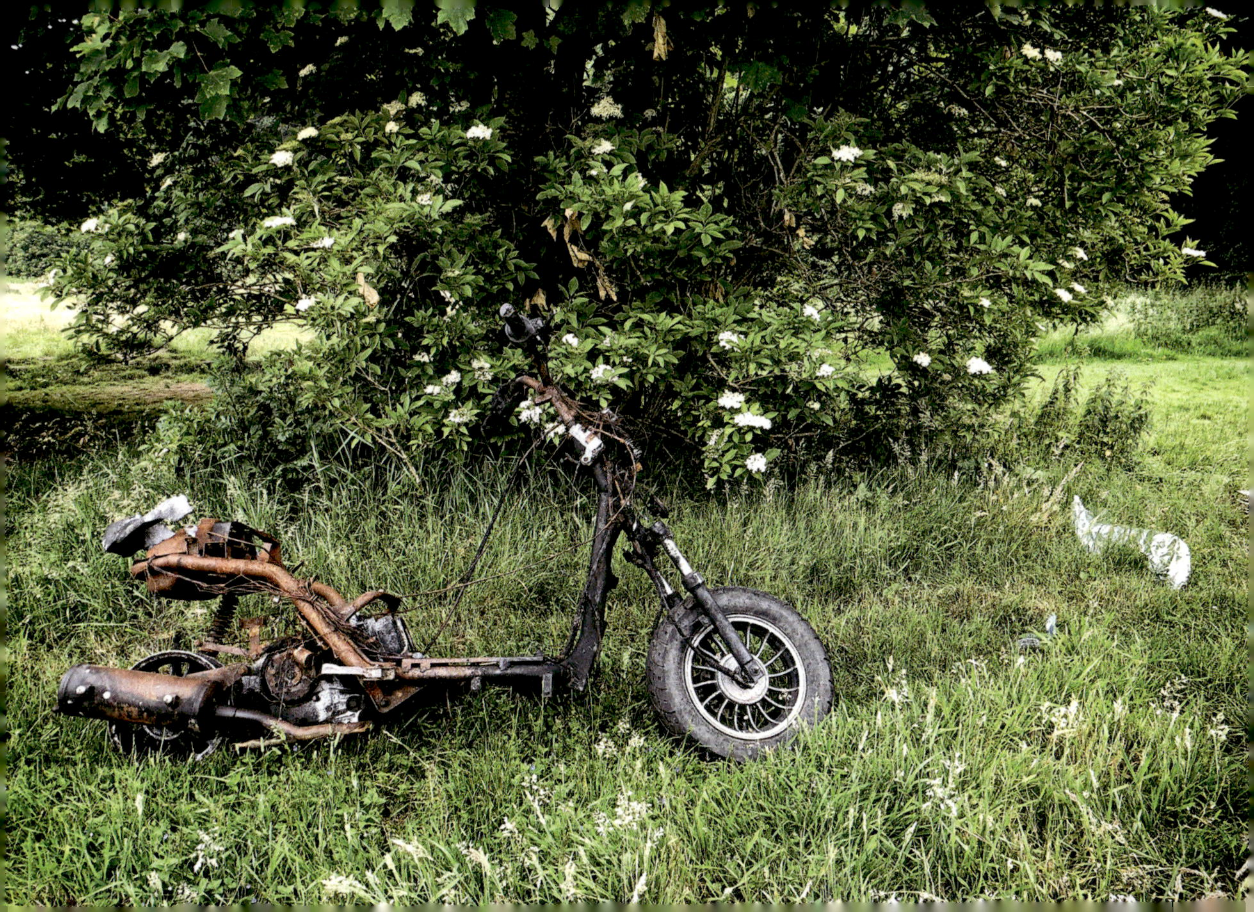

No Sleep Till Seafield

As aspirational slogans go, 'Stay up forever' is quite good. Yet forever is quite a long time. I worry what children would do at Christmas – how will Santa sneak into their bedrooms if they are fully alert and reading Nietzsche's *Thus Spake Zarathustra*? Who will bolster the bolster industry? Where will the bogeyman live if it is not underneath the unwanted bed?

Beware, for all things have consequences.

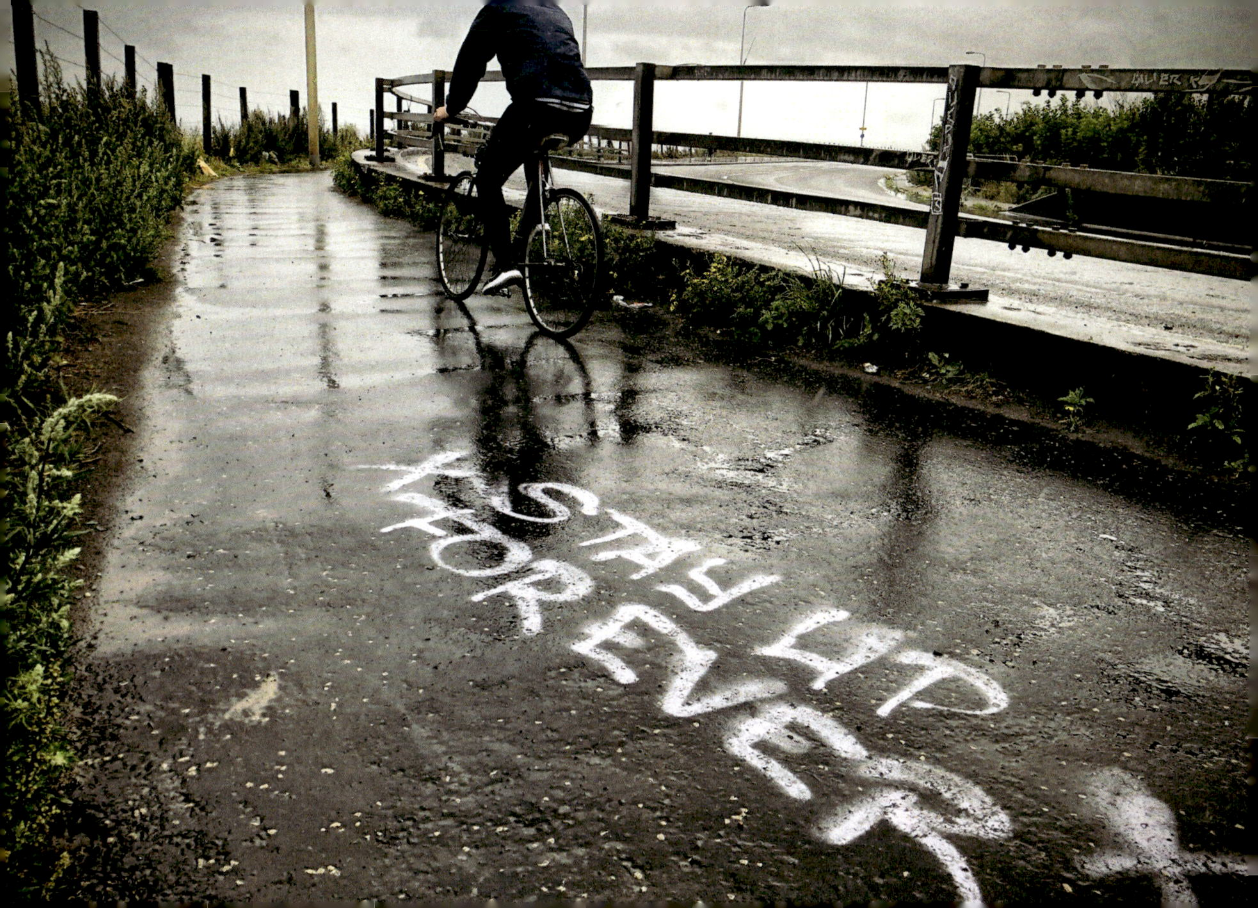
STAY HIP
FOREVER

The Lonely Sound of A Train Whistle By The Sea

Cold grey concrete by a cold grey sea may sound dreich, but to be there with the needle-sharp wind bringing every sense to crystalline acuteness and to hear the squealing and squawking of the gulls and the low eternal rumble of the sea is one of the great pleasures of coastal cities.

We build these concrete structures to last. The sea laughs at our plans.

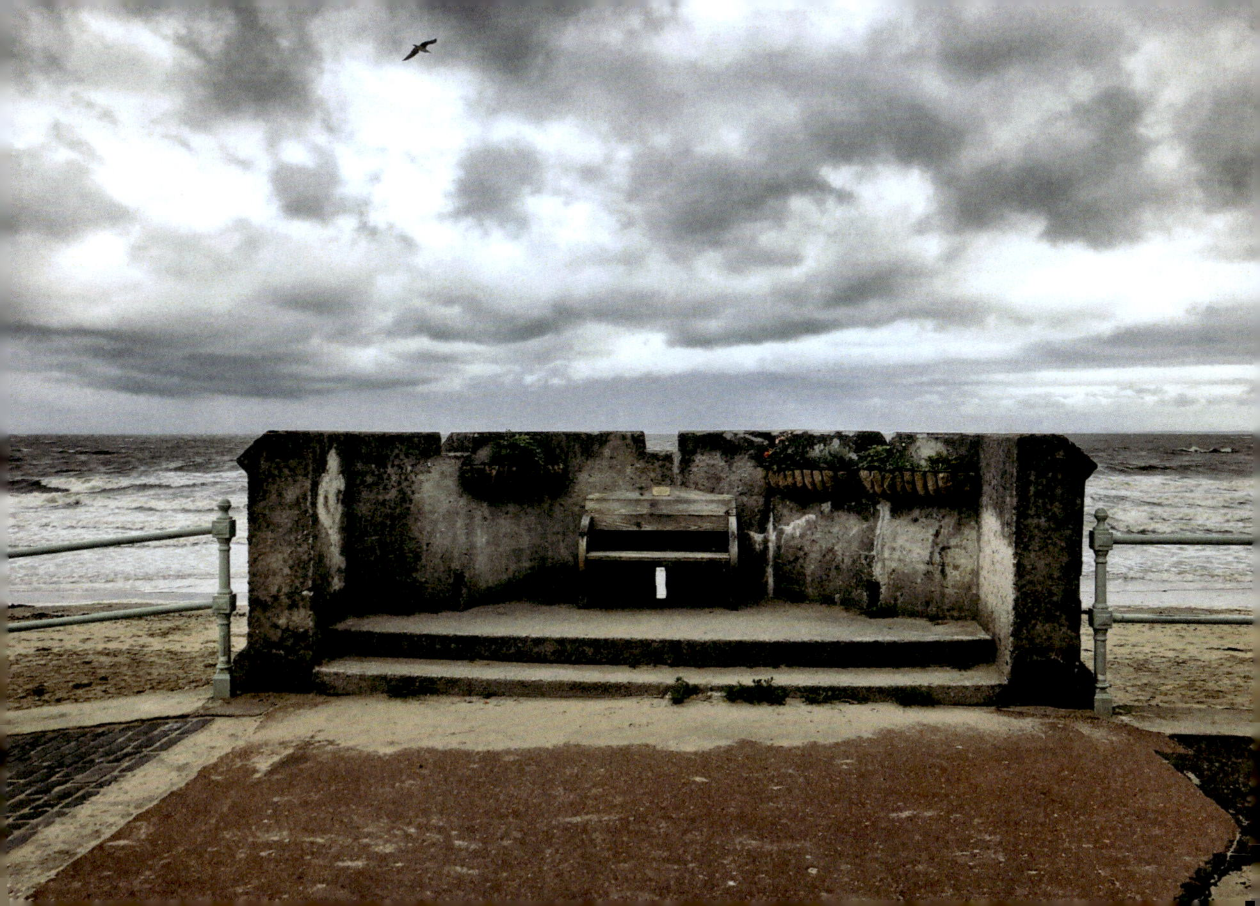

Once Upon A Time In The South(side)

Fixed myself a mess o' beans, slung on my gun belt and six-shooter, saddled up my Appaloosa and headed on down the range to Dodge. In order to do so I took care to avoid the venerable elderly matrons of Morningside (a fearsome foe more frightening than Jesse James himself).

Lassooed myself a sarsaparilla before galloping off into the sunset (well, drove home to Leith, to be more accurate).

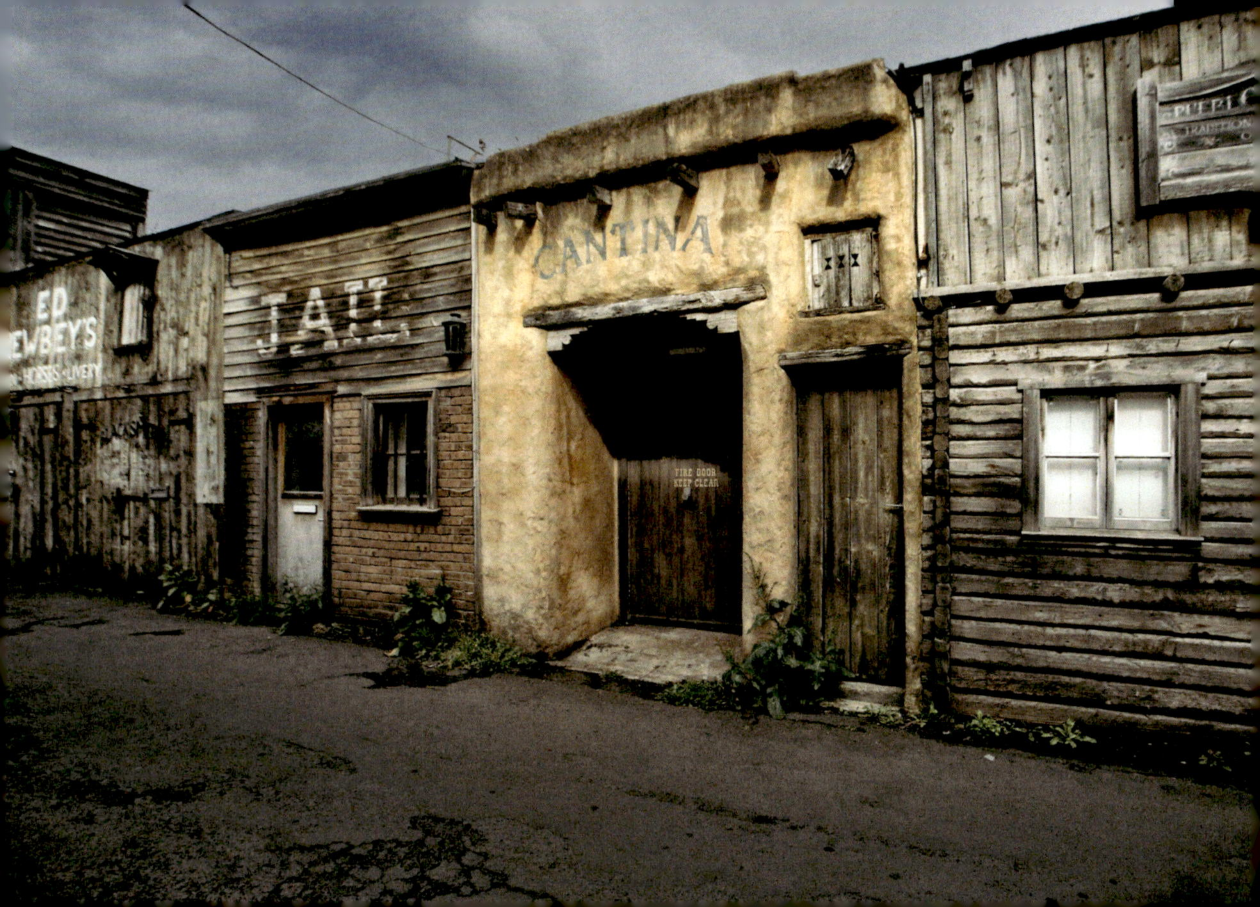
ED
EWBEYS
HORSES LIVERY
JAIL
CANTINA
FIRE DOOR
KEEP CLEAR
PUEBLO
TRADITION

Together In Electric Dreams

It was the great hope of the mid-1980s that almost everyone derided
– the Sinclair C5. To be fair it was a bit rubbish, but as a beautiful piece
of hopeful idealism it is hard to match. It predated the mass move to
electric vehicles by decades and although the technology wasn't ready
the idea was, and without ideas there would be no technology.

And they still look great.

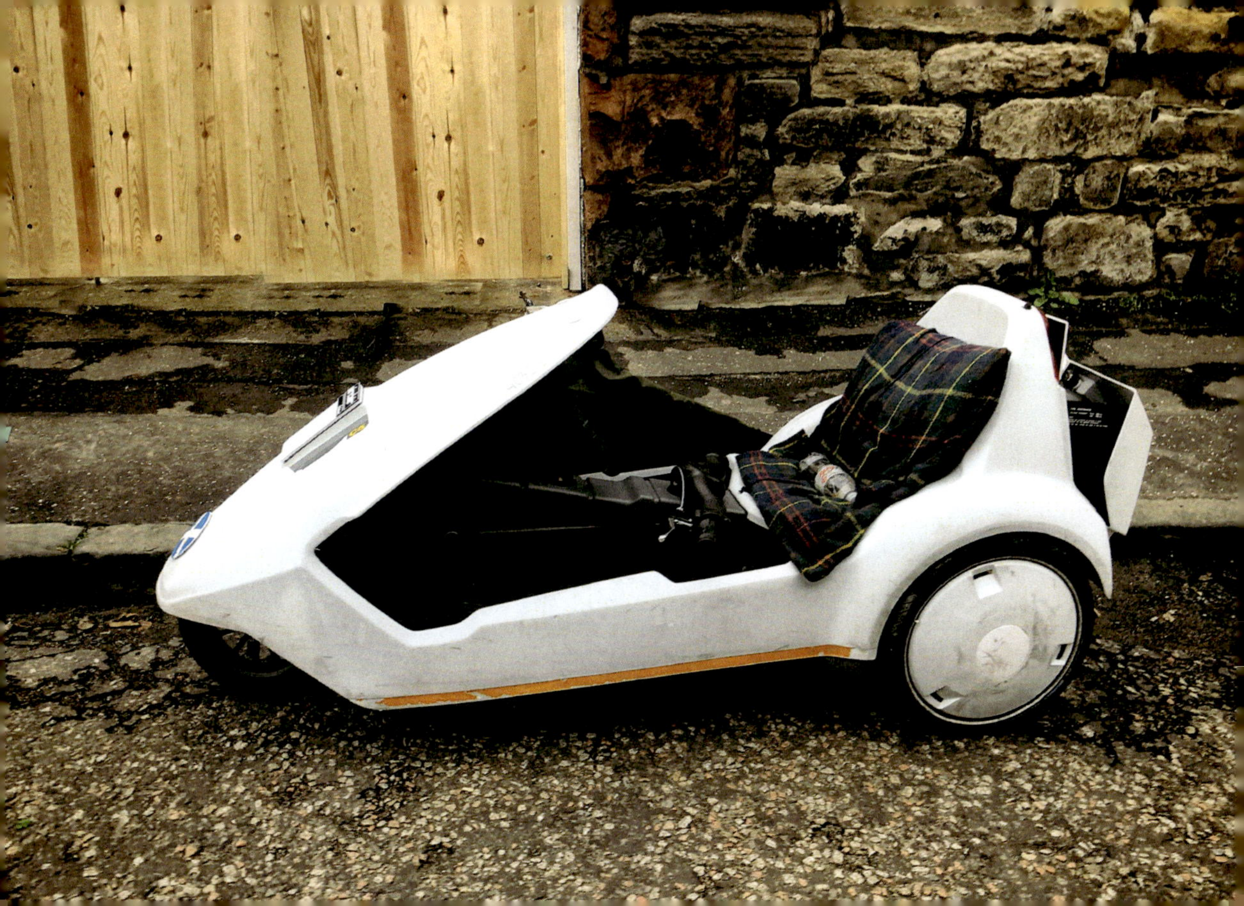

Those Long Postdiluvian Days

Nobody told the water where it had to stop. We build banks and fences and position benches to sit and watch the widlife, and the water comes to have a look at all these structures and sails happily on by.

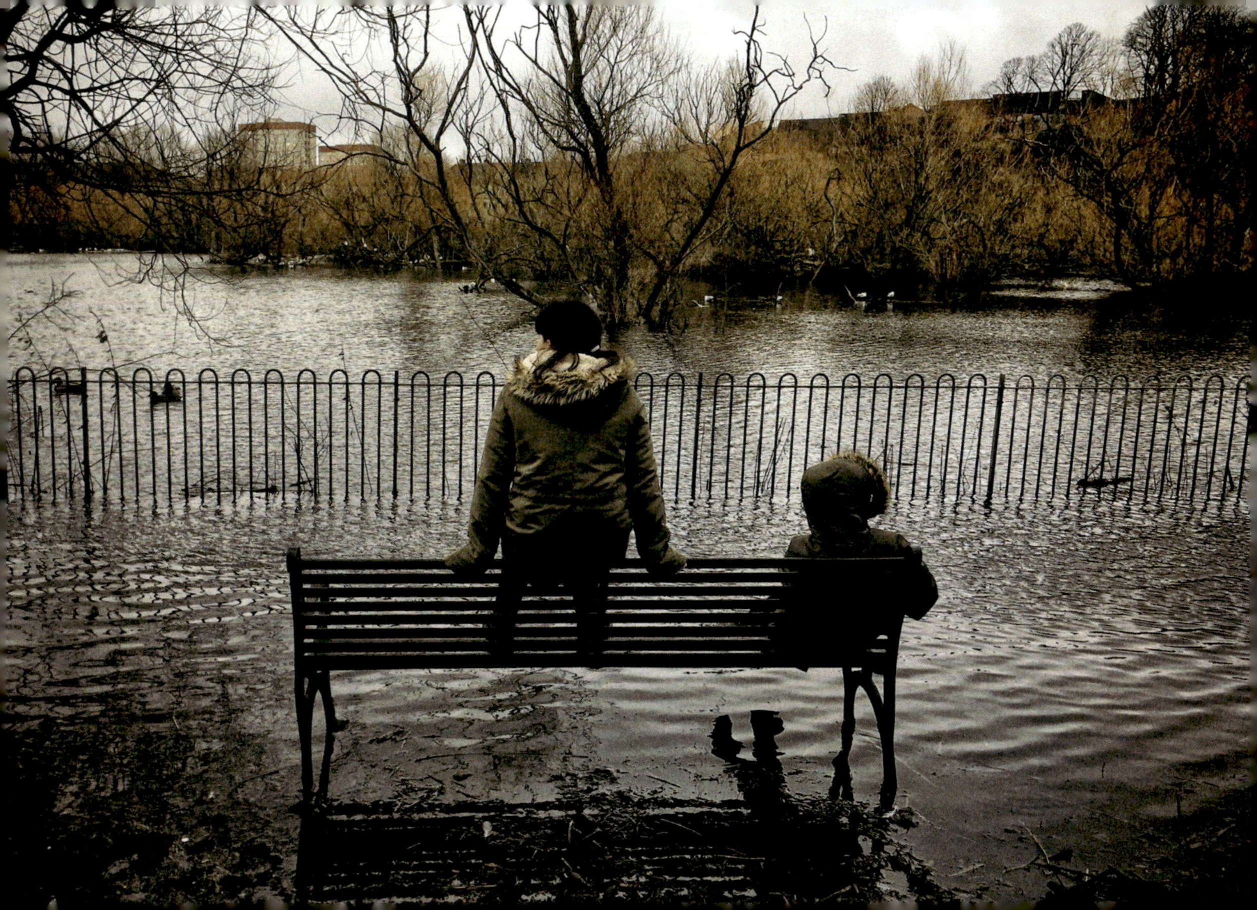

New People Arrived From Other Lands

It may be that the advertising budgets for Audi have been slashed, or it may be that discerning car thieves wouldn't be seen dead with those tyre brands. Either way it's not really something you see every day (unless you work in Kwik Fit).

For the record my money is on four wormholes connected to faraway galaxies, although the tyres were a bit smelly so I never tested that theory…

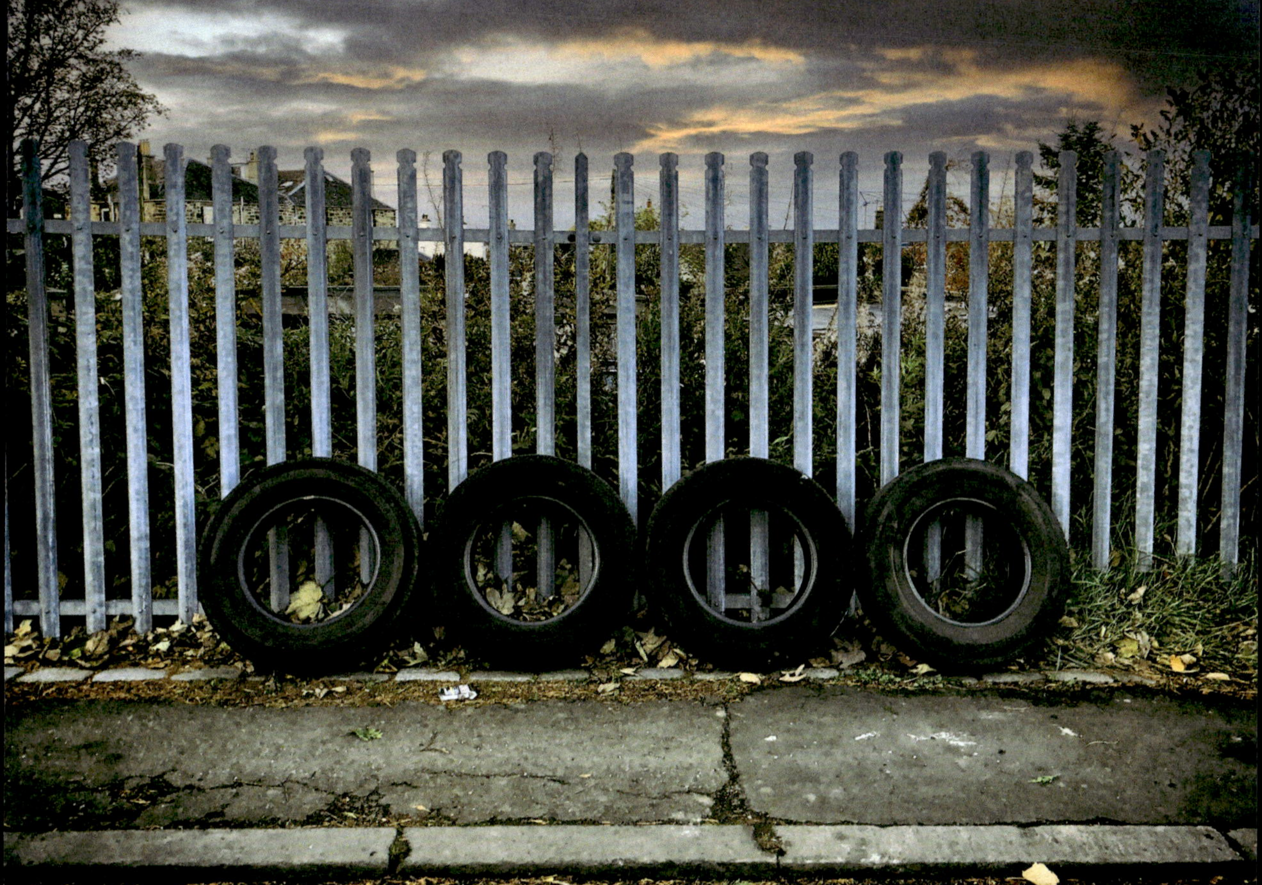

The Green And The Grey

If you were looking for an image to illustrate the dictionary definition of dreich this would surely be it. A damp that chills to the core, a day that never brightens and a gloom as deep as watching Scotland crash out of another major footballing tournament.

My favourite kind of day (apart from the Scotland losing bit).

I Lingered Round Them, Under That Benign Sky

A cold evening approached as unbended, we ascended. Suddenly over the crest of a small rise, on that bleak hillside, two crosses appear. What funereal place is this, with only harsh grass and biting wind as mourners?

As we approach, our viewpoint changes. The two crosses reveal themselves as two wooden chairs. A resting place for weary travellers, but not the final one.

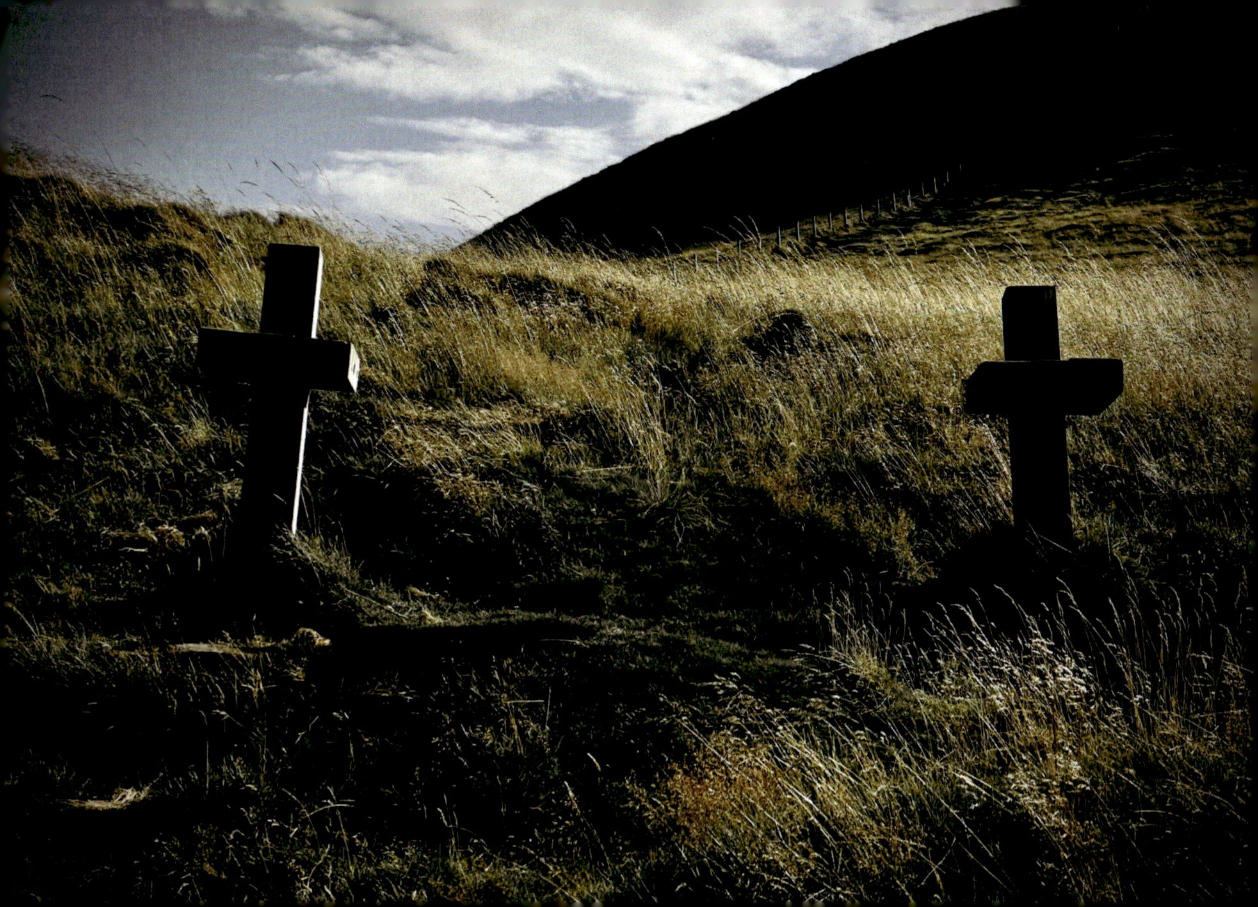

The Last Dying Rays Of Civilisation

As the sun begins to set on those short winter days, and the ground is rimed with frost, what a delight to catch the lights, chimes and stale diesel of the unexpected ice cream van. It is never too chilly for a Mr Whippy.

'99, sir?'
'No, just the one, thanks.'

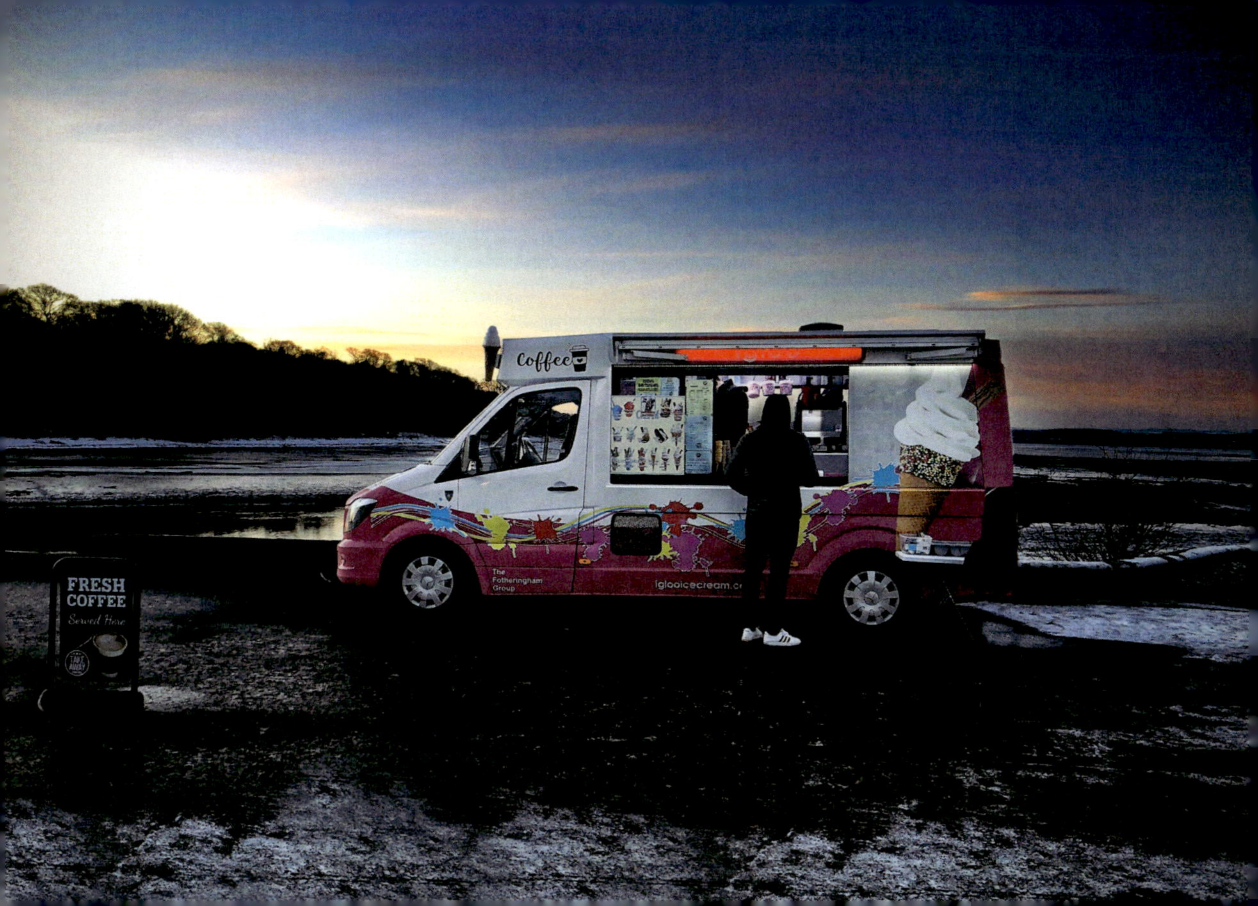
Coffee
FRESH COFFEE
Served Here
TAKE AWAY
The Fotheringham Group
iglooicecream.c

The Flags Are All Dead At The Top Of Their Poles

There is a beautiful, still, cold, damp dreichness that on lucky days we can huddle together in. And then there is this type of dreich. Hard, bitter, dismal with a lack of hope. This is Princes Street on a Saturday afternoon in early 2020 during the first lockdown. No trams, no buses, no noise, no people.

What happens after people?

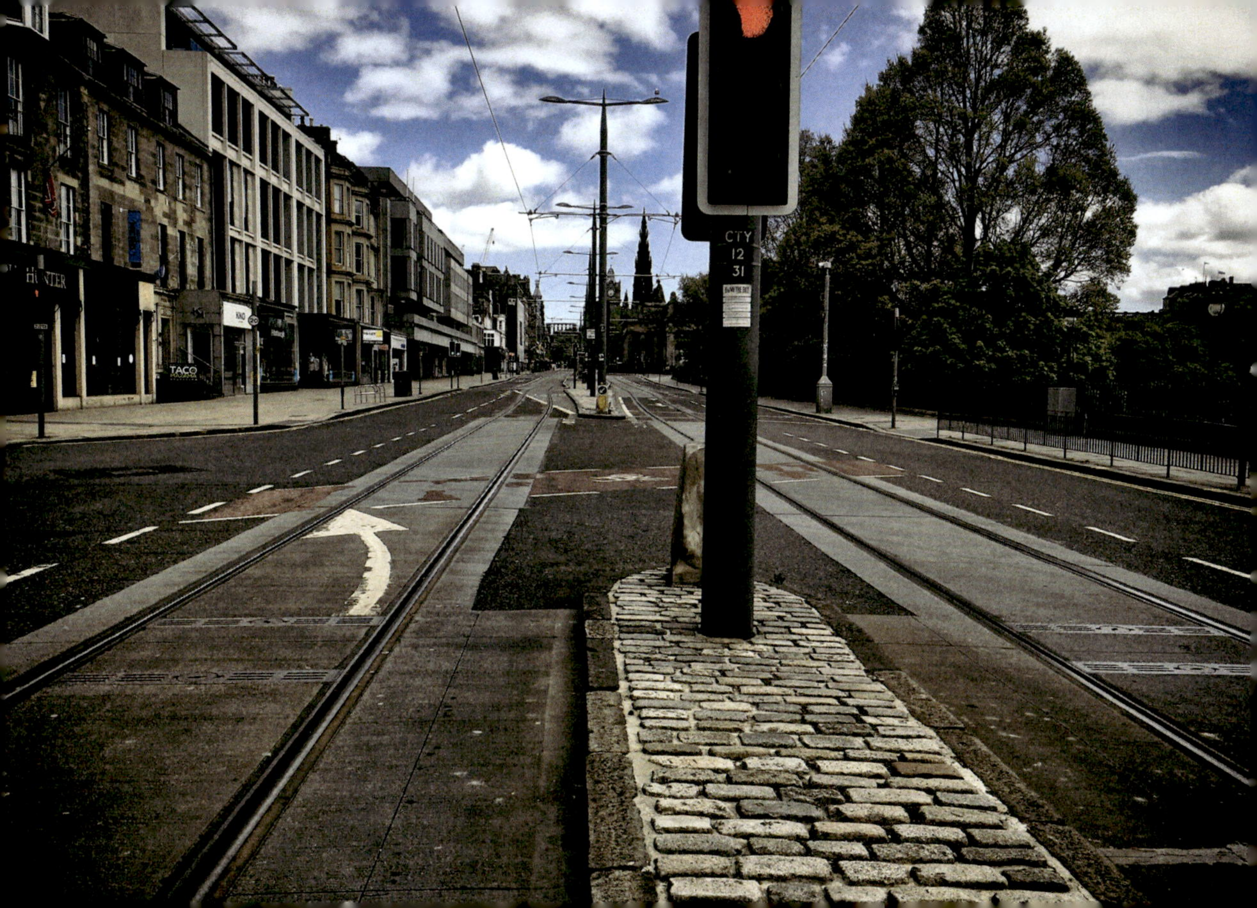
HUNTER
TACO
CTY
12
31

The Sound Of Distant Engines

It's every child's football nightmare.
The ball lost behind the impenetrable barbed-wire topped fence,
more vicious than any forest of thorns that hid Sleeping Beauty's castle
for that long century.

Come back in 100 years, kids, and the fence will magically open.

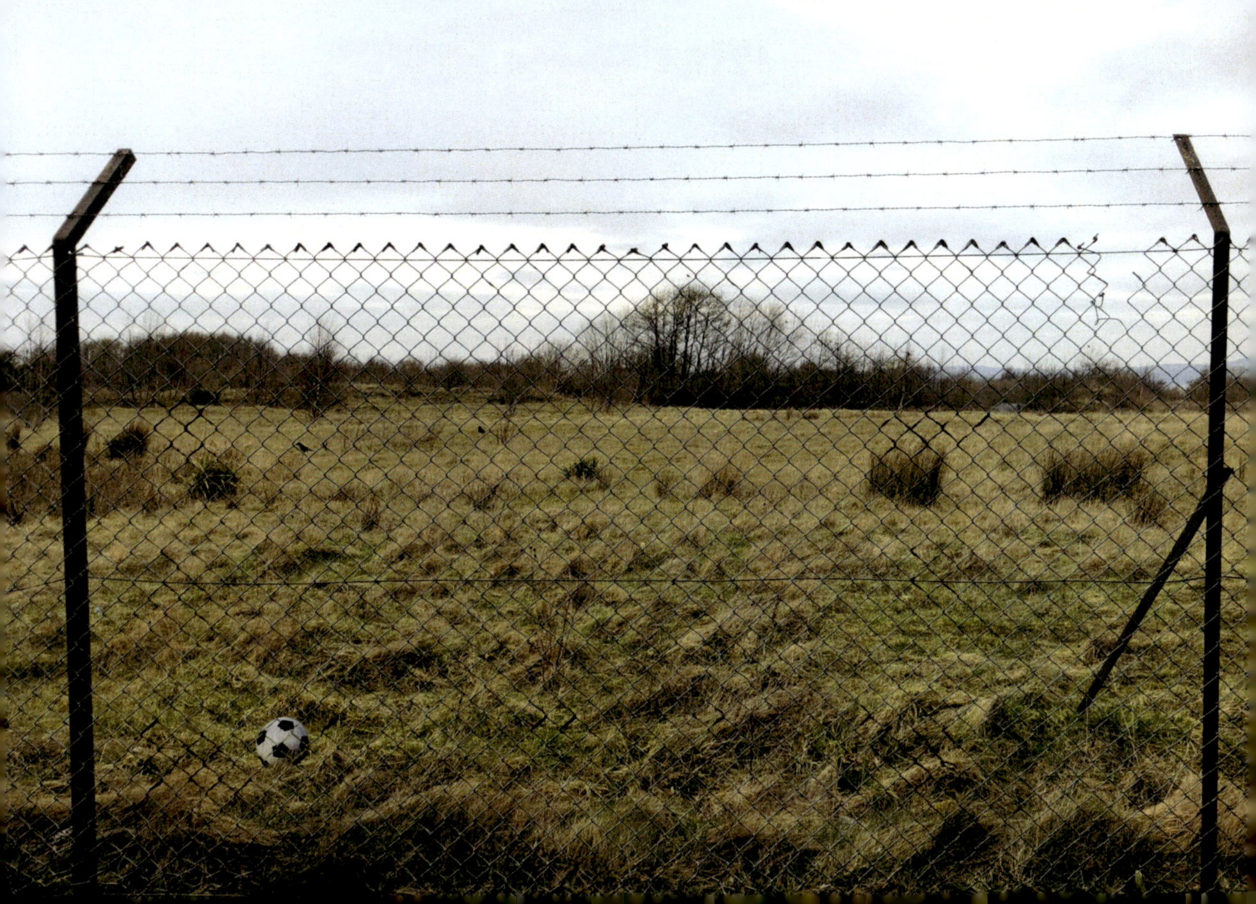

There Is No Water Only Rock

What secrets used to lie inside these great grey concrete monoliths?
No surface clue or hint is ever given. Huge structures that massively sit
and, like Smaug, jealously guard their secrets, reminding us that once
these places mattered.

Once noise and clamour reigned within.

All silent now, watching.

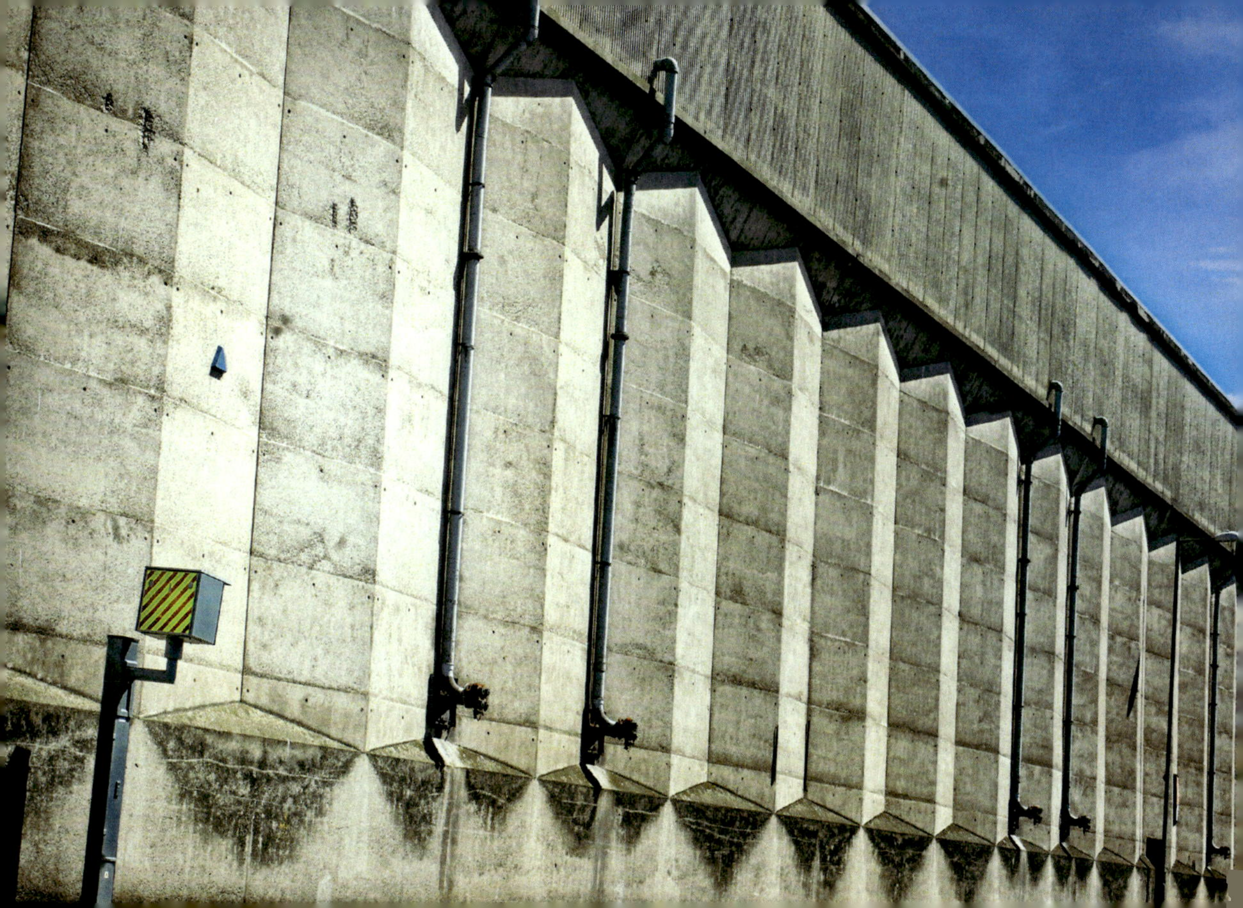

Stars Like Songs Across The Skein Of Space

A supplicant sentinel bows beneath another Edinburgh sunset. Dark, ponderous and heavy like a summer storm at night, these twilight gifts punctuate the long months of winter and provide a brief glimpse of colour and light before the long dark begins.

Rain Falls On A Windless Evening

Wet cobbles lead beneath darkening buildings on a rainy autumn evening. From overhead the sound of a night train charging south to the morning. Then silence, broken only by the sound of footsteps, your own, as you disappear quietly into the outer dark.

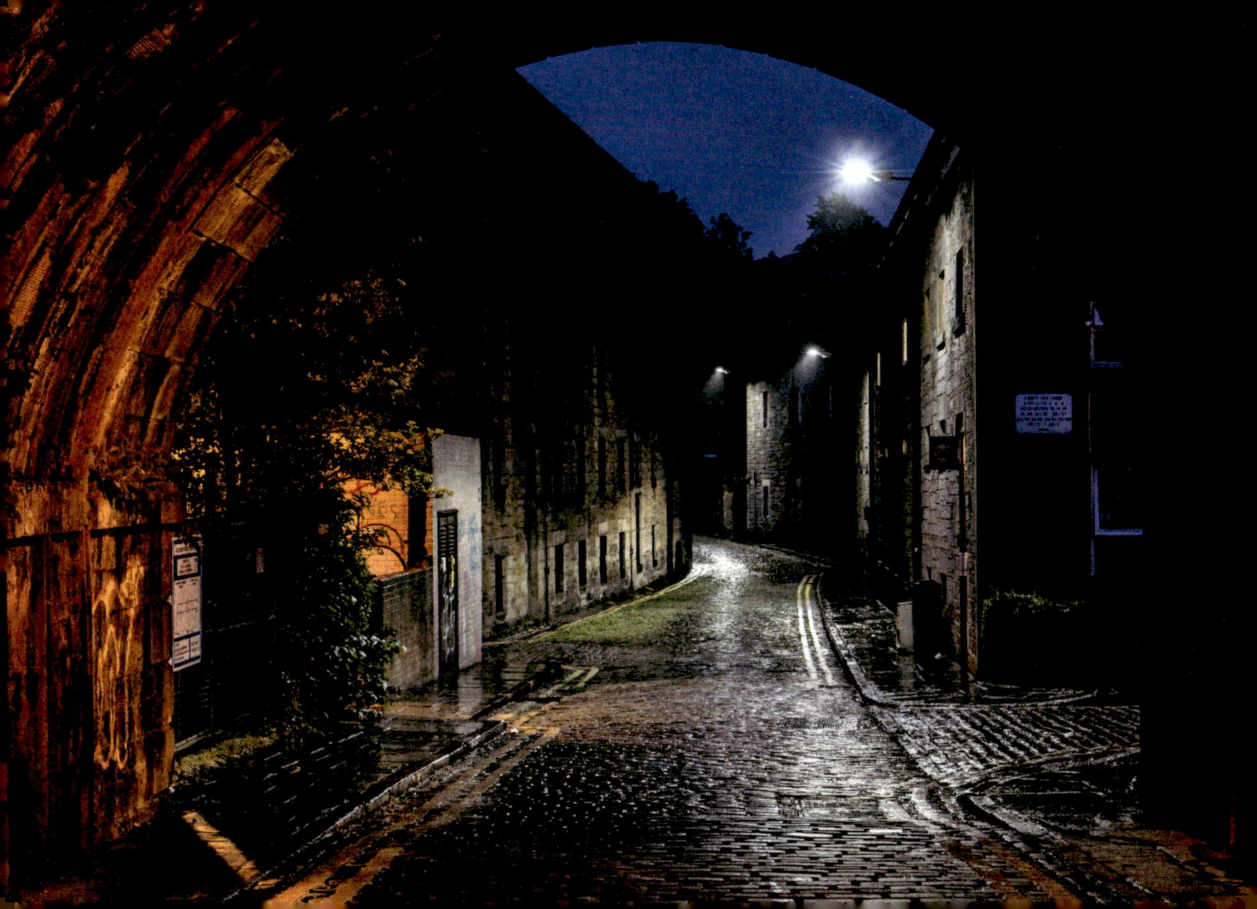

The Silver Light That Transfixes

Opened in 1930 as The New Victoria cinema, and known as The Odeon from 1964 until its closure in 2003, this lovely Art Deco cinema is now mostly gone. The facade and foyer remain but the main and smaller auditoriums havebeen demolished, replaced as part of the unending feeding frenzy that is the construction of student accomodation.

How many heroes or villains shone down from that screen?

Progress is good, but things get left behind.

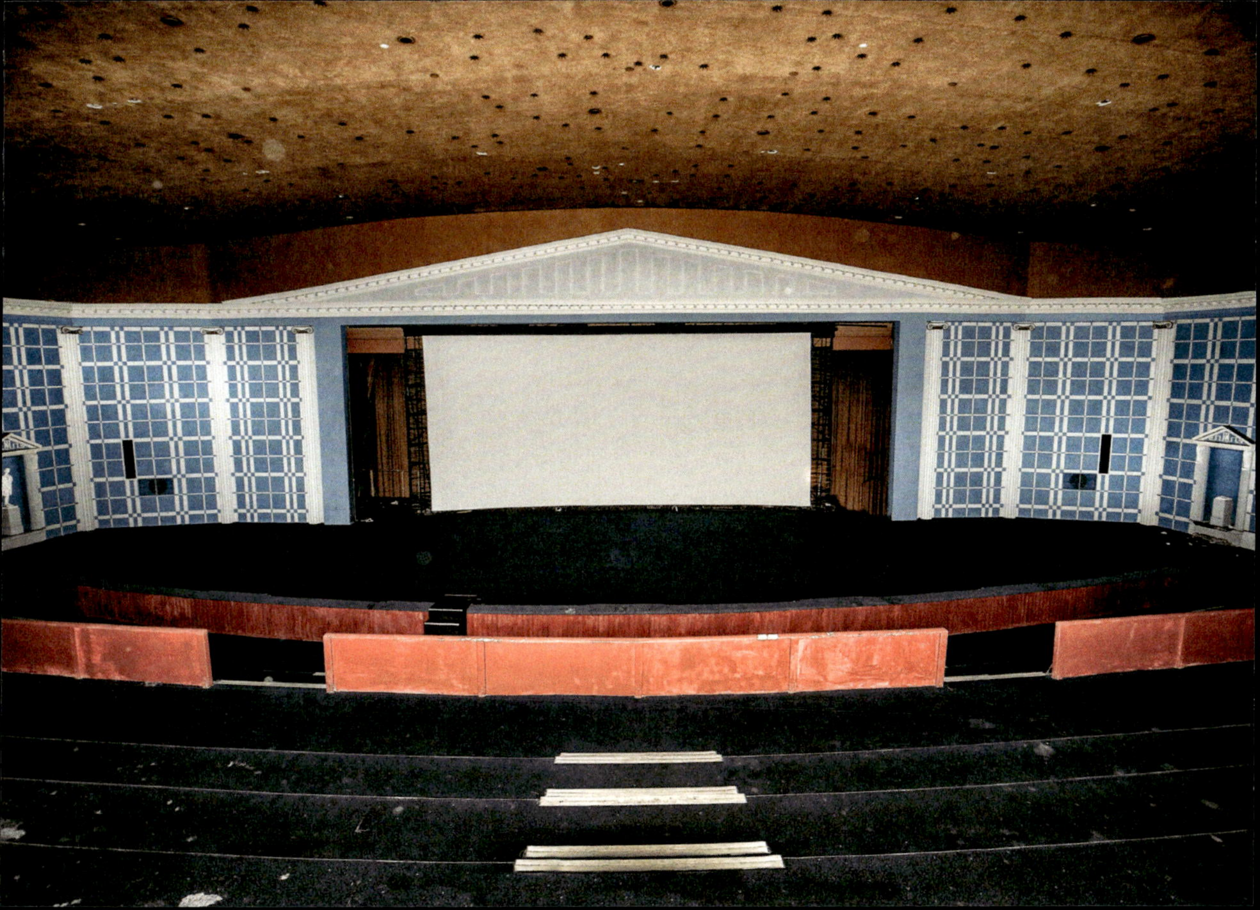

Skies That Fade Behind A City Block

Is there anything so dreich as boarded-up homes? What stories could these buildings tell? What joys and delights, tears and dramas took place behind those walls?

All quiet now though, as only the wind whispers its truths in quiet, dark rooms.

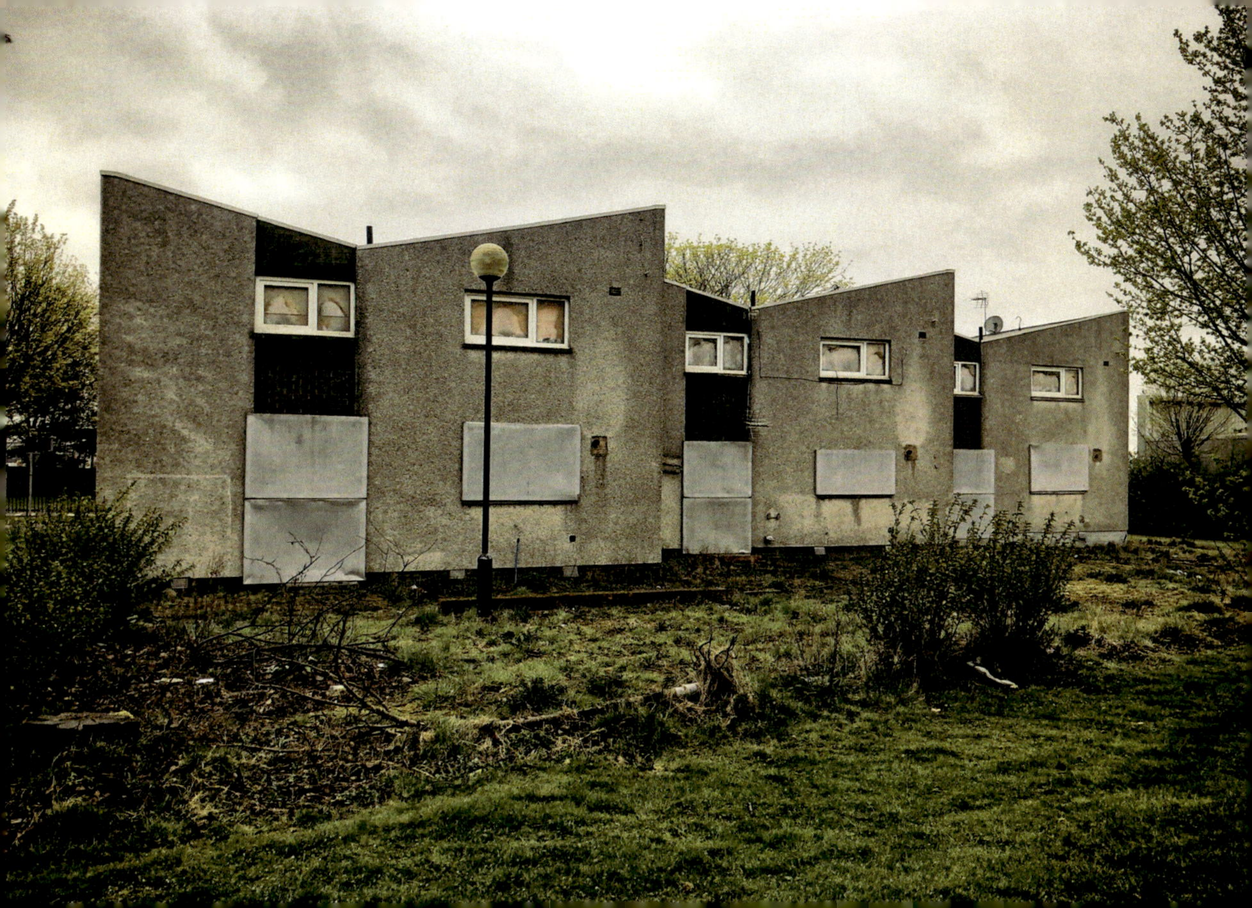

It's A Concrete Jungle Out There

Shape, angle, form, pattern.

Combine them with metal, concrete and tarmac and you are living the brutalist dream. These future dreams all look tired now. The glittering utopia neverdid match the ones on the architect's drawing board. And yet the idea was pure, let down by those eternal destroyers of dreams, practicality and money.

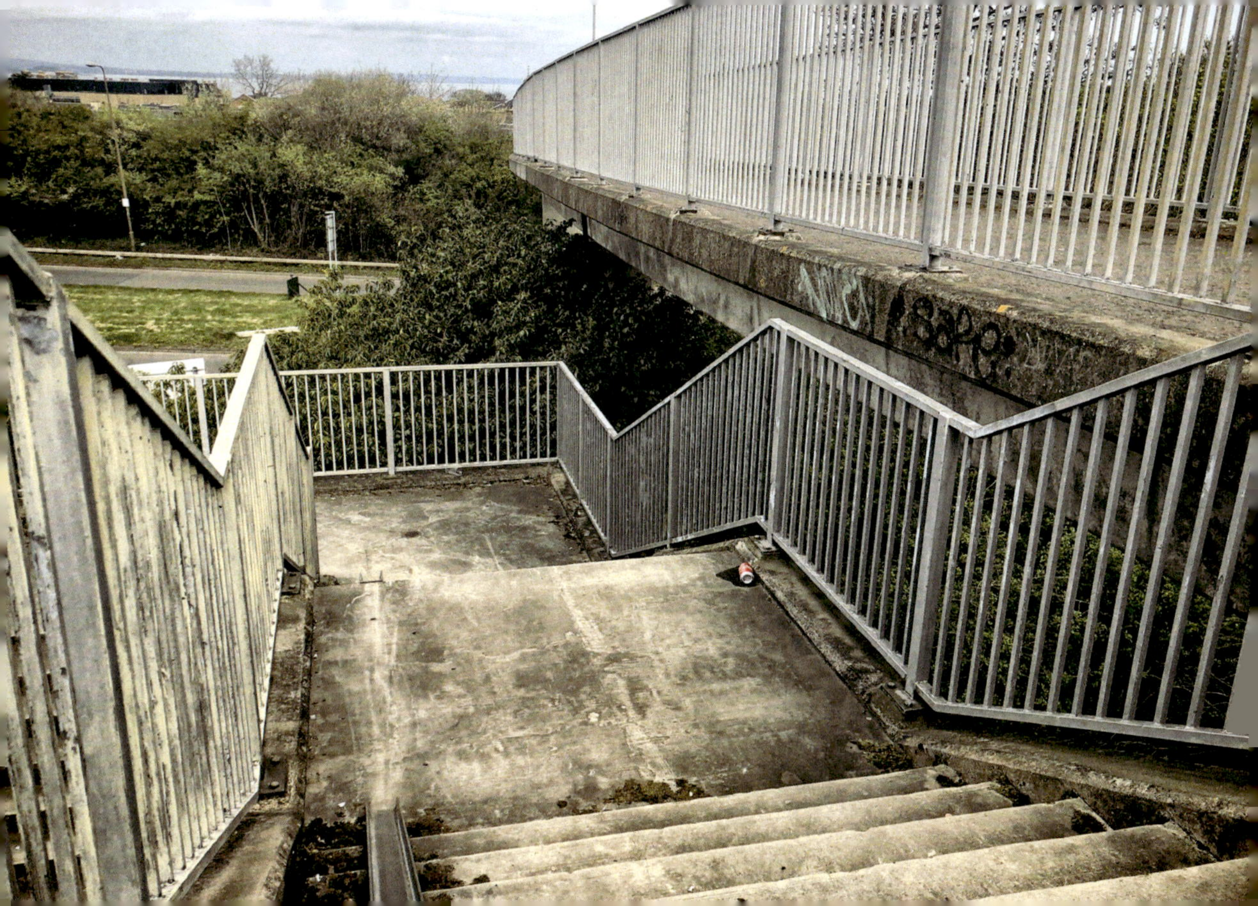

An Absence Of Youth Is Not A Youth Of Absence

The skate-park lies quiet and empty, resembling a giant dinosaur excavation site from where all the bones have long since been removed.

No screams or dreams of children today, for we are still deep in the grip of this icy pandemic that suffocates the chance to play and stifles the acrobatic wishes of skater and roller-blader alike.

It will pass though, it will pass.

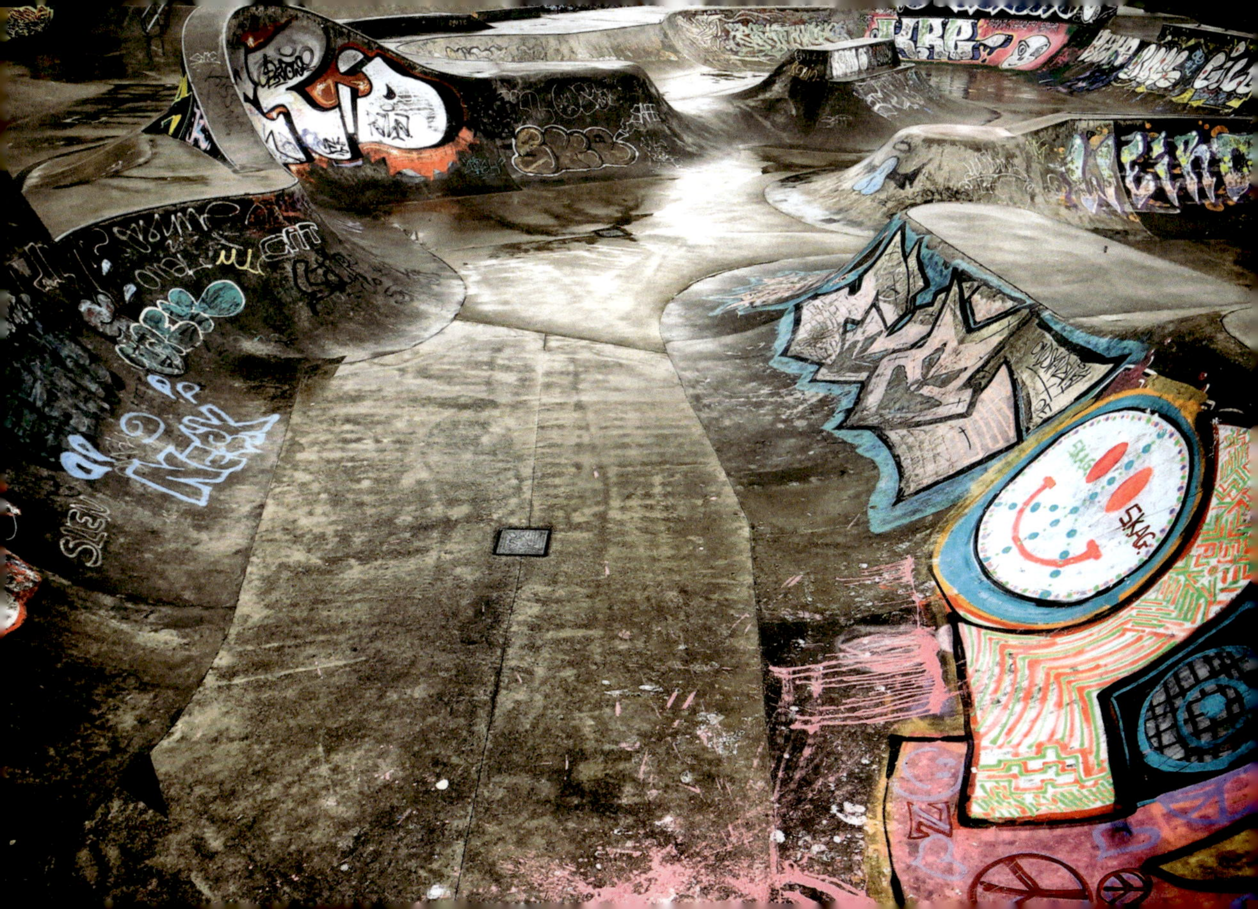

Winter Kept Us Warm, Covering Earth In Forgetful Snow

'The game's off!'

In 1978 the snow on the pitch would have been a minor issue. Scrape
the snow away from the lines, get out an orange ball, spray the Deep
Heat on and away you go.

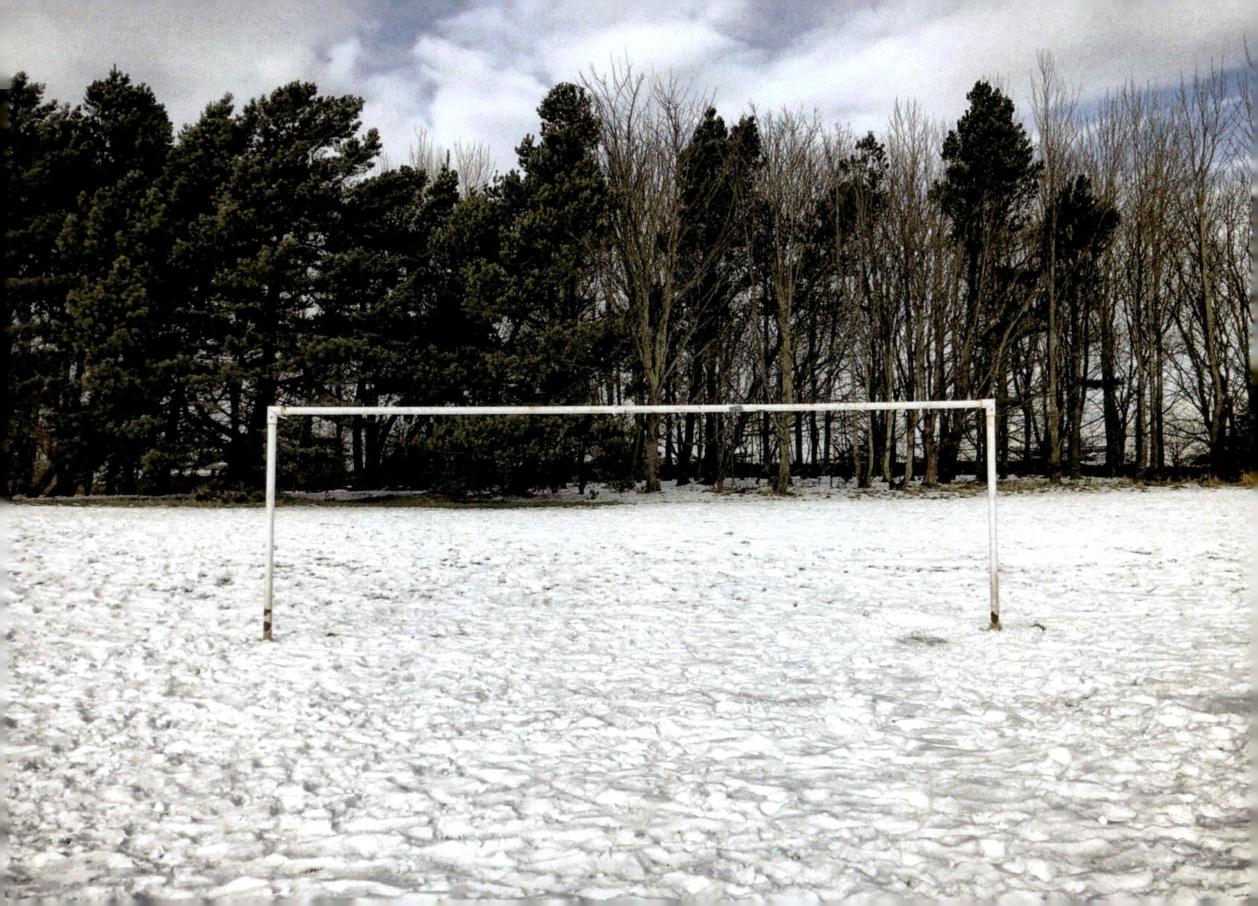

Dirty Old Town

One day all this will be gone. The massive concrete sea defences, the car-dealerships, the sewage works, the ramshackle industrial buildings that pepper the coastline from Cramond to Joppa.
All of this will be gone.

And in its place who knows what? No doubt it will be clean, and regimented, and shiny for a while (before the sea demands its tribute).

And even though I know it's wrong, I will miss this beautifully ugly seafront.

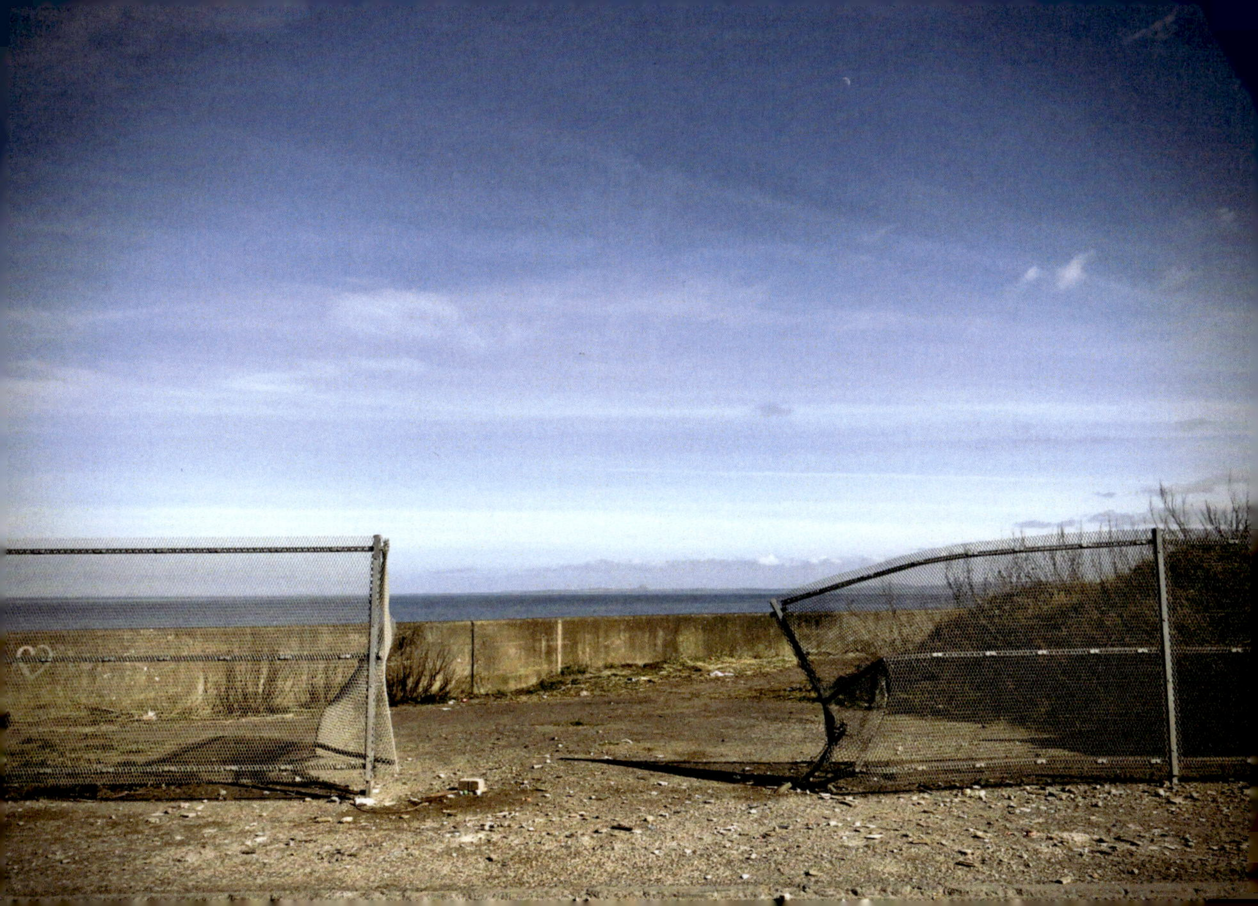

A Time Of The Signs

No it's not a sign from outside either Tynecastle or Easter Road Stadiums...

It is the curse of children everywhere – that patch of green, usually entirely deserted that is deemed more worthwhile to be left empty than to resonate with the shouts and laughter of kids.

We always ignored them anyway.

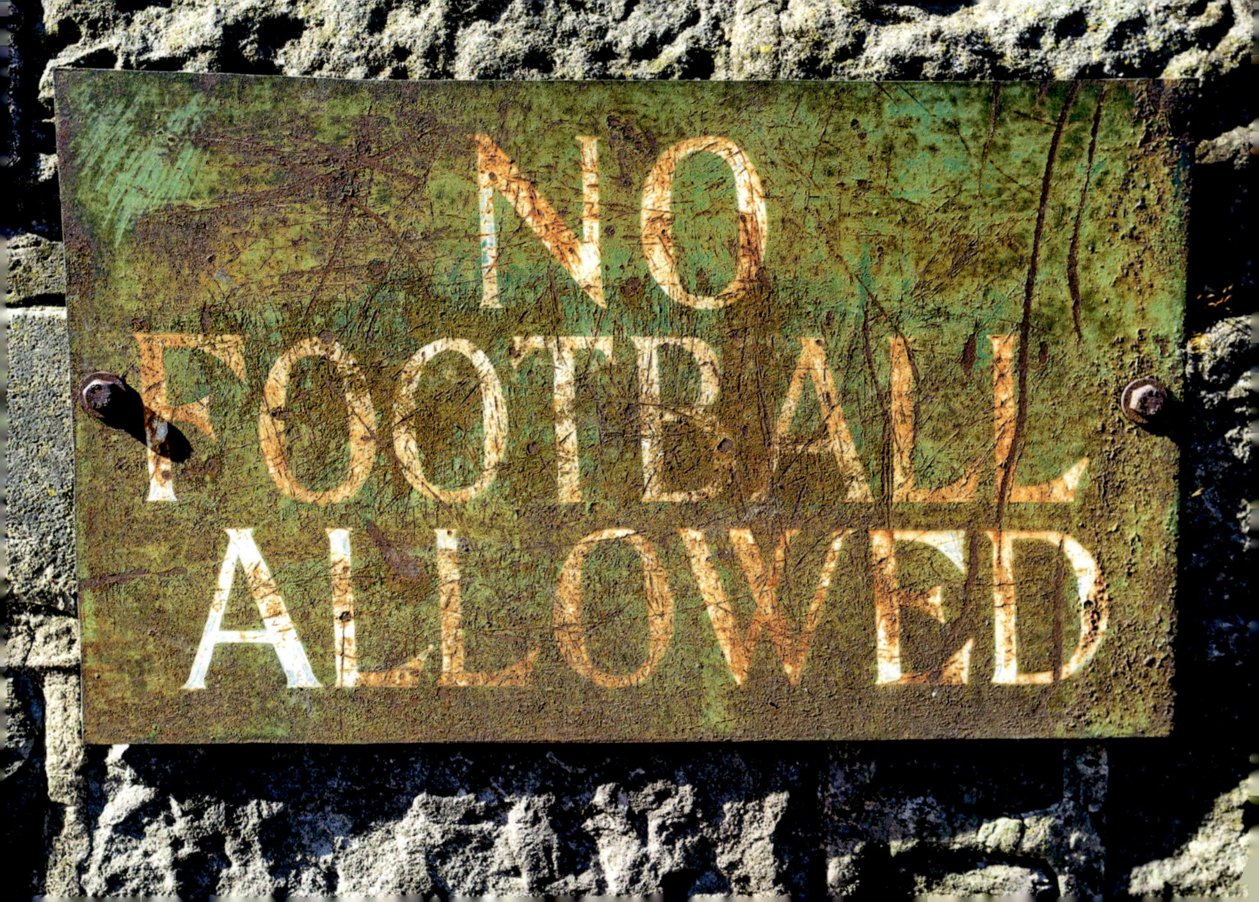

NO
FOOTBALL
ALLOWED

How To Build Impossible Structures

One person's monster is another's angel. Of the many beautiful buid-
ings in Edinburgh this is my favourite. Everytime I walk past I wonder just
how it manages to stays up.

'Science, innit?'

And yet to many, this building and buildings like it are unwanted ugly
beasts – monstrous carbuncles in fact. However, these people are simply
wrong and need to be incarcerated in a concrete factory and forced to
repeat the phrase 'I love Brutalism and it loves me' until the end of time.

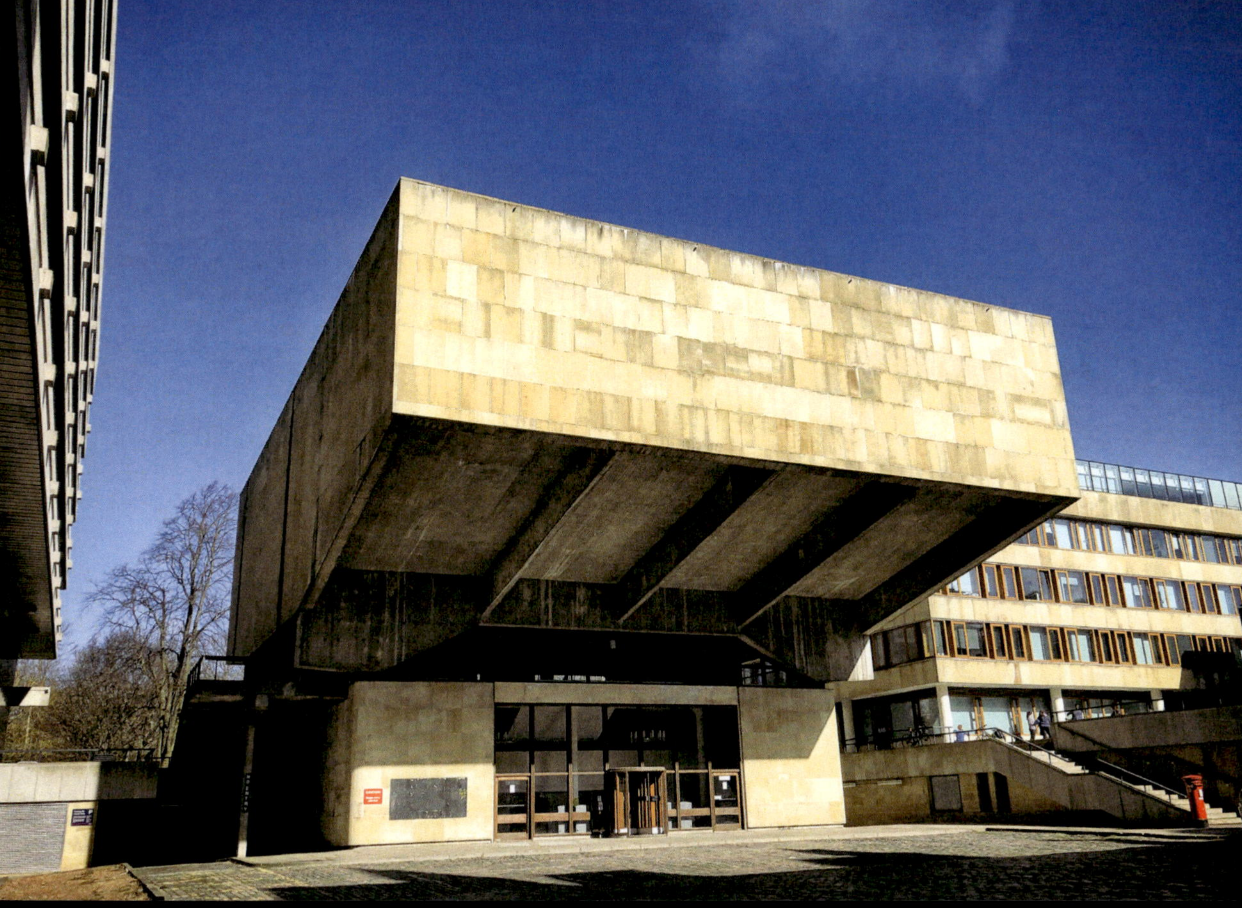

The Grime That Gathers At The Rim Of The World

And verily did the Lord say unto them 'Affix thy number plate
correctly and refrain from parking beneath the bough that is heavy
with the flying beasts of the sky.'

Imagine sauntering into a drive-through car wash in that? It would take more
than a top of the range Hot Wax & Sudz wash to clean that bad boy.

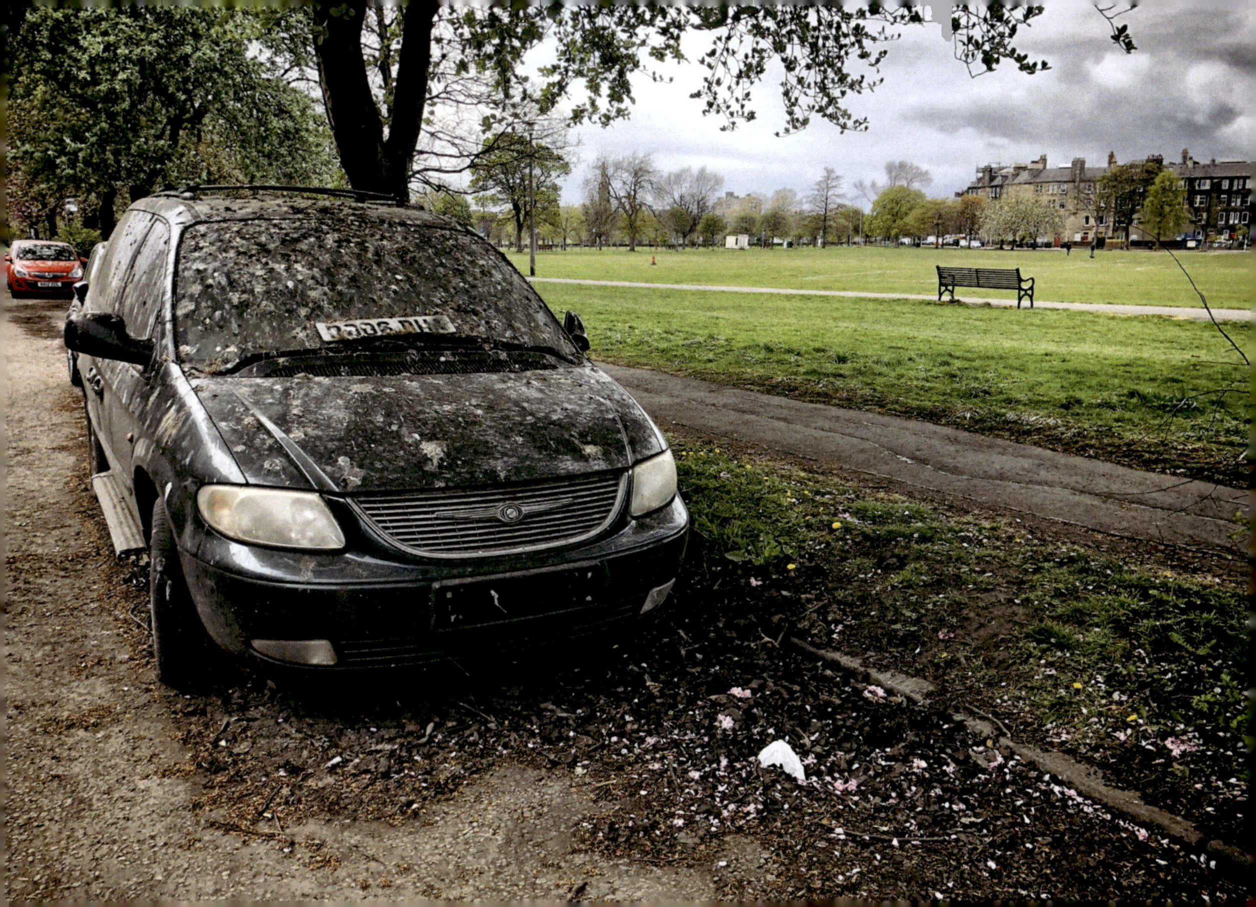

Welcome To The Apocalypse Playground!

Not once, in years of passing this park, have I ever seen a child in it. Occasionally my own small child will, with the same curiosity that sends people bungee jumping off cliffs, venture carefully in. After an unsatisfying series of bumps down the un-slidy slide he will wander out again saying, 'Daddy, can we go the park?'

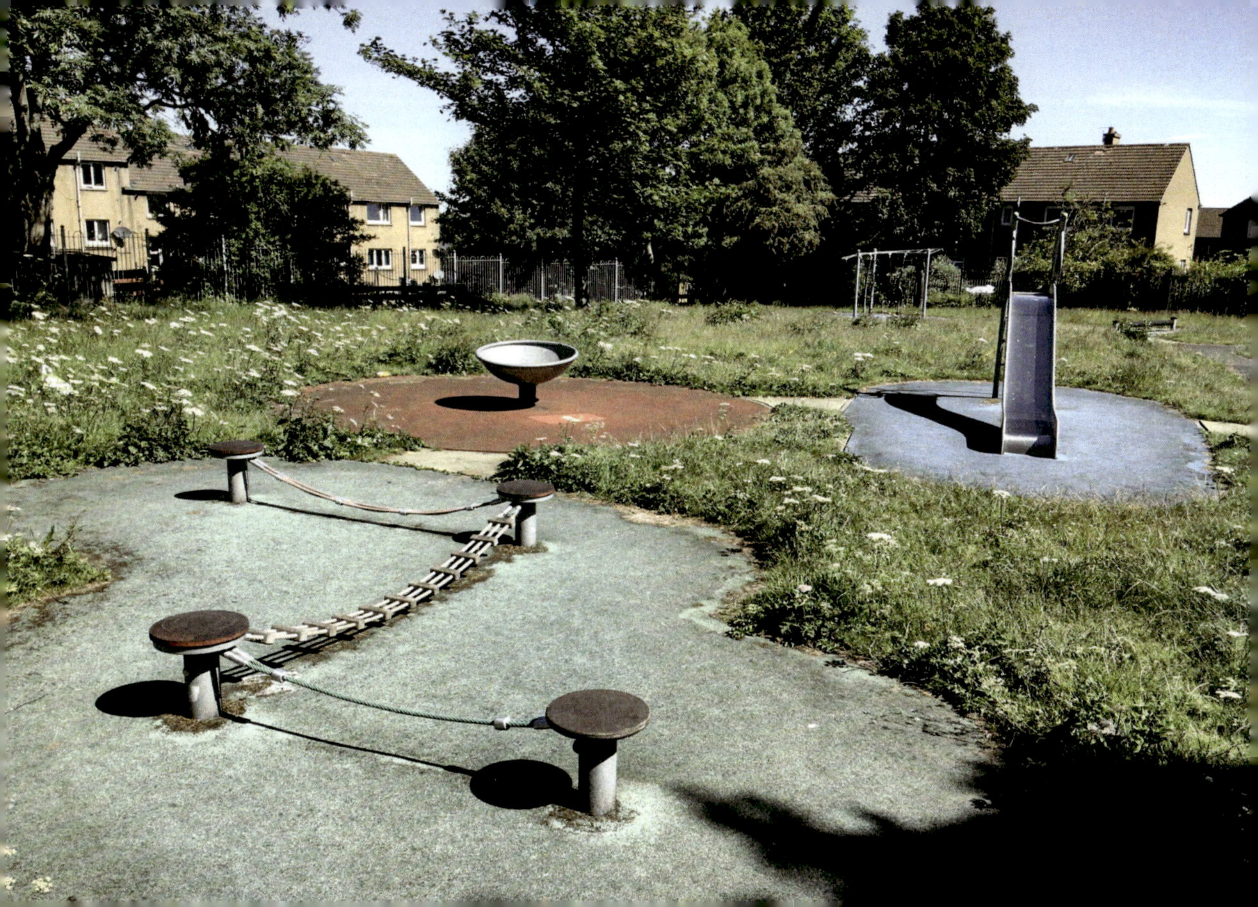

An Evening Redness In The West

We knew we would miss them when they were gone. Rising high above the east end of Princes Street they stood a lonely guard over the new development that replaced the old St James Centre in Edinburgh. Every night they would come to a rest in a different position, and silently semaphore their gibberish message to the stars.

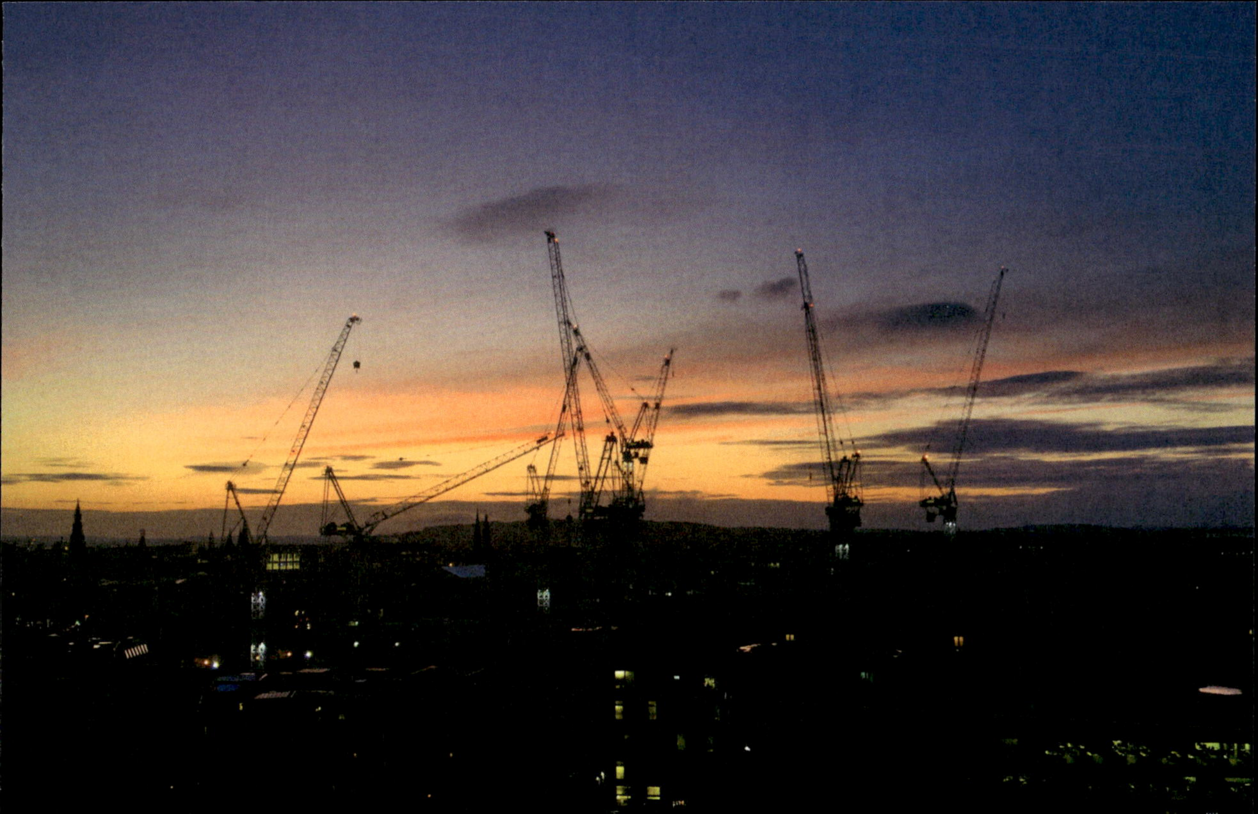

To Stare At Seas Long Gone

Should we give them the benefit of the doubt? The hugely popular Scottish comedy series *Still Game* had an episode where one of the main characters bought a cheap doormat, with the word Welcome spelled Weclome. I think we can show faith in people and decide firmly that this the joke here.

And if it was an accident? Well, I think I might rather be weclomed than welcomed anyway.

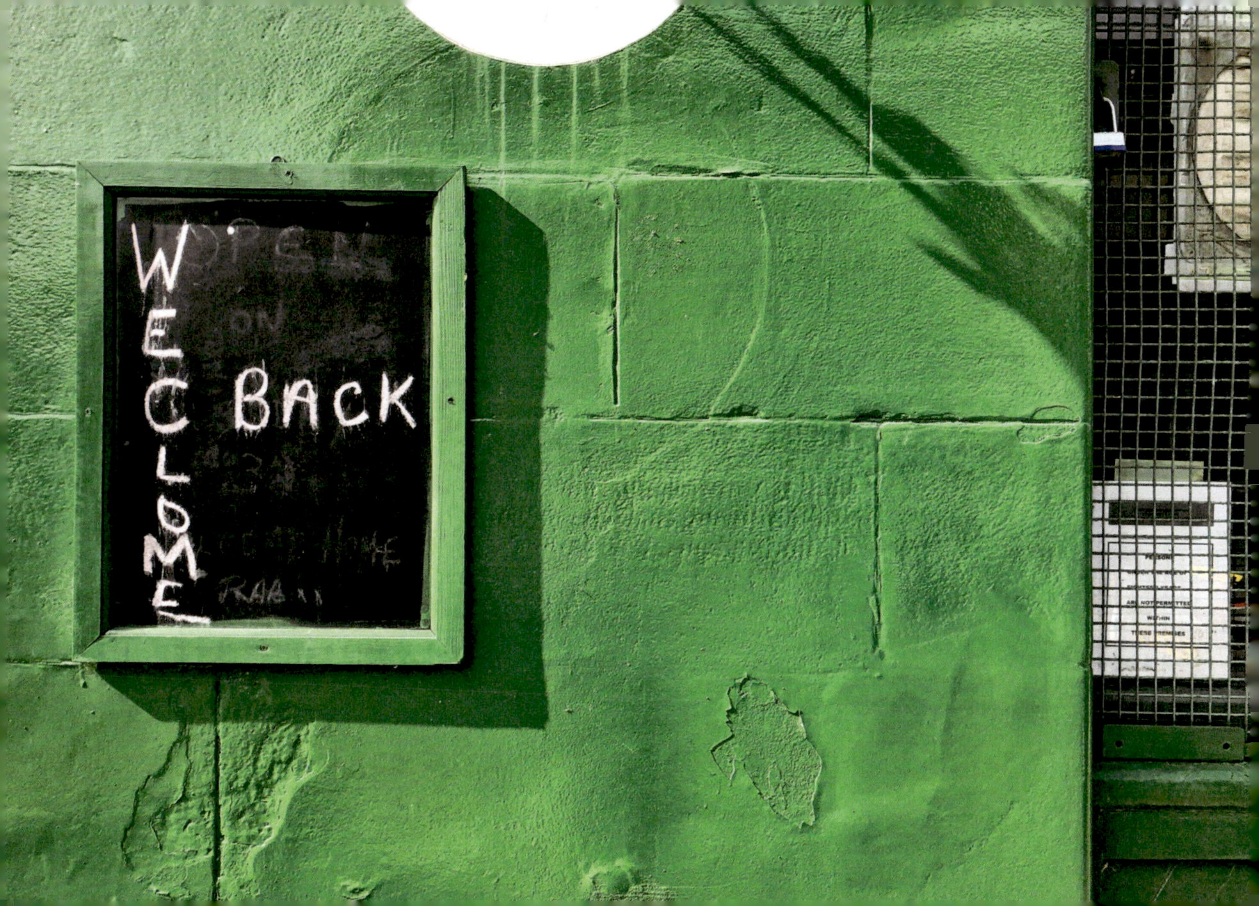

WELCOME
BACK

Dark Shapes That Loom In The Night

A picture that could adorn a thousand dreary shortbread tins. Castles always look better in bad weather as they suddenly appear, squat and menacing, out of the gloom. They weren't designed to look pretty but to be a projection of power and a reminder of who was in charge.

I much prefer Edinburgh Castle when it looks like this –
a fever dream of a Gothic novelist.

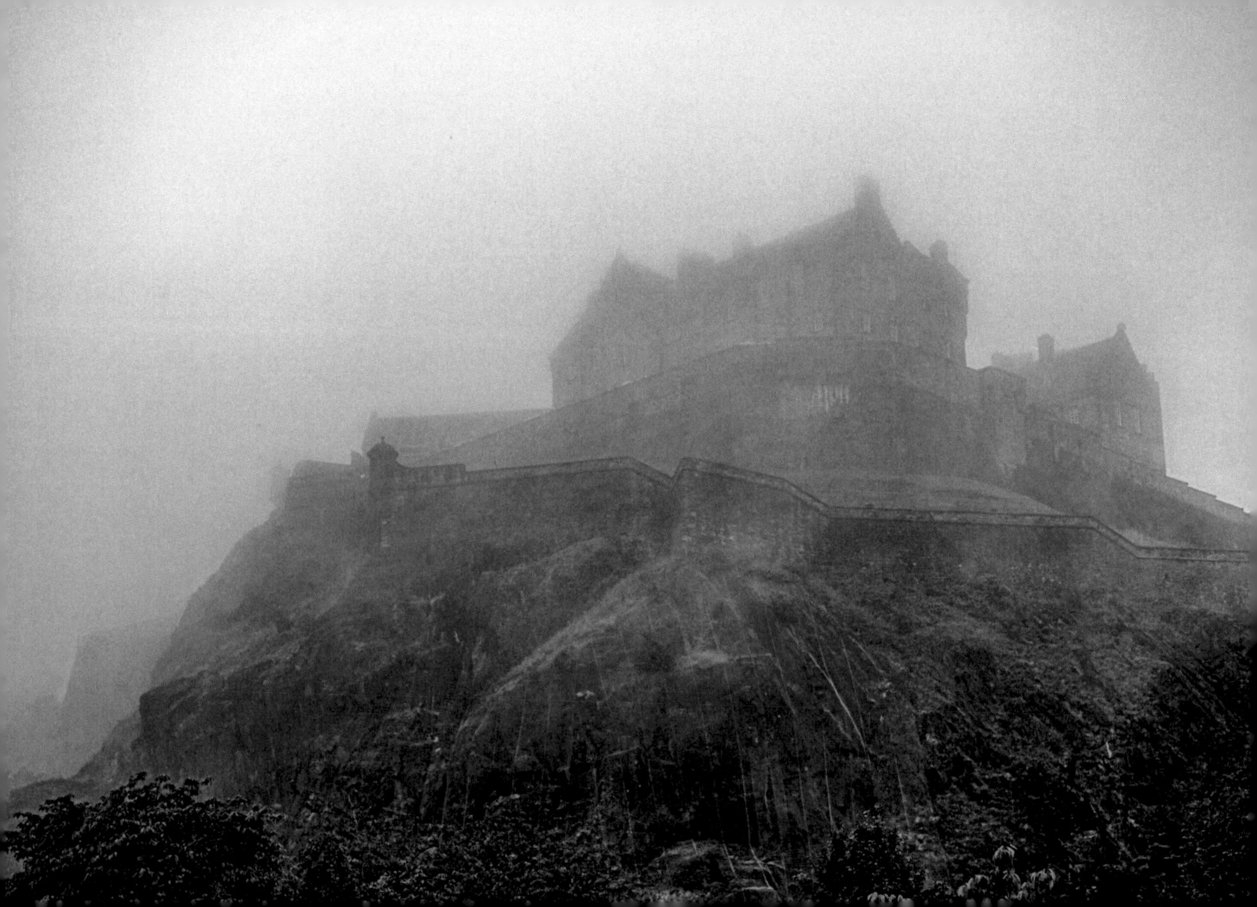

The First Picture Of You

What's going on here then? This lovely old Lotus Excel has taken a battering – still looks in pretty nice shape though (sadly the same can't be said for the old boat behind it).

I wander past whispering 'The Lotos eaters in Elysian valleys dwell.'

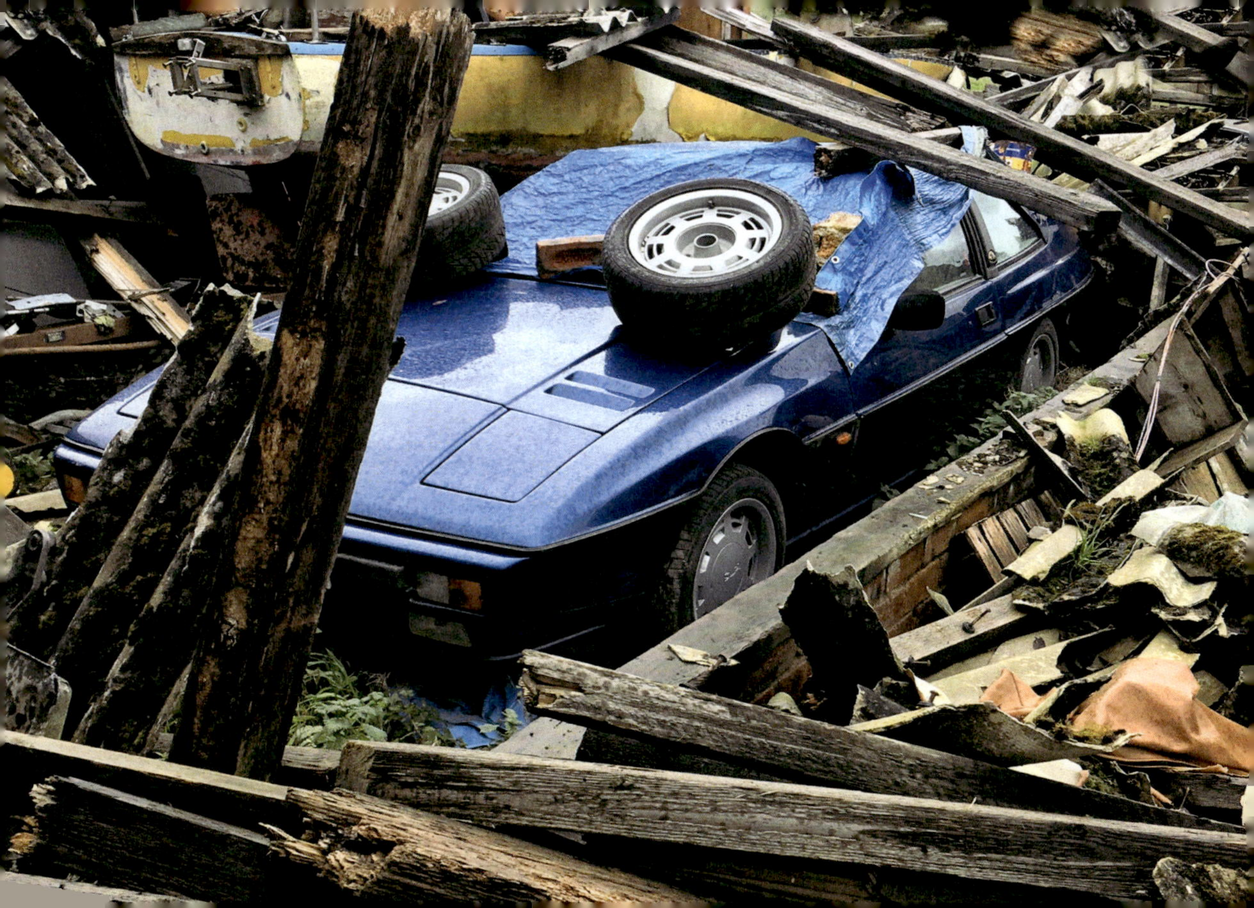

Heard It Through The Grapevine

Such a good idea. Although in my student days I used to love a trip to the launderette. Always warm and nothing to do for about an hour, except sit and read or watch the world go by. Where did that free time go?

Of course, an outdoor launderette in winter isn't the best place
for a Nick Kamen strip…

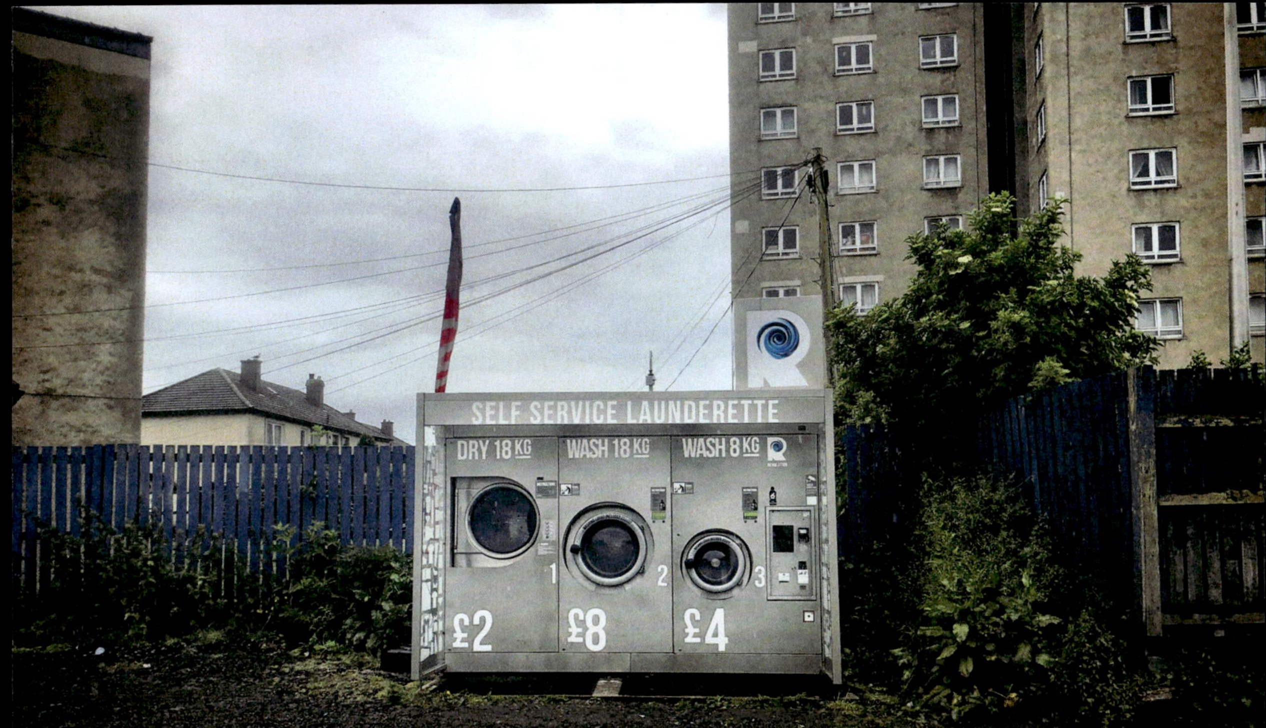

SELF SERVICE LAUNDERETTE
DRY 18 KG
WASH 18 KG
WASH 8 KG
1
2
3
£2
£8
£4

We Find Our Way By The Fires In The Sky

You know that the world is dreich when a visit to the dump feels like a day out. During parts of 2020 when everything else was dormant one of my few pleasures was a satisfying declutter and trip to the recycling plant. That's how bad things were…

And just occasionally the sky puts on a show as if joining in the fun.

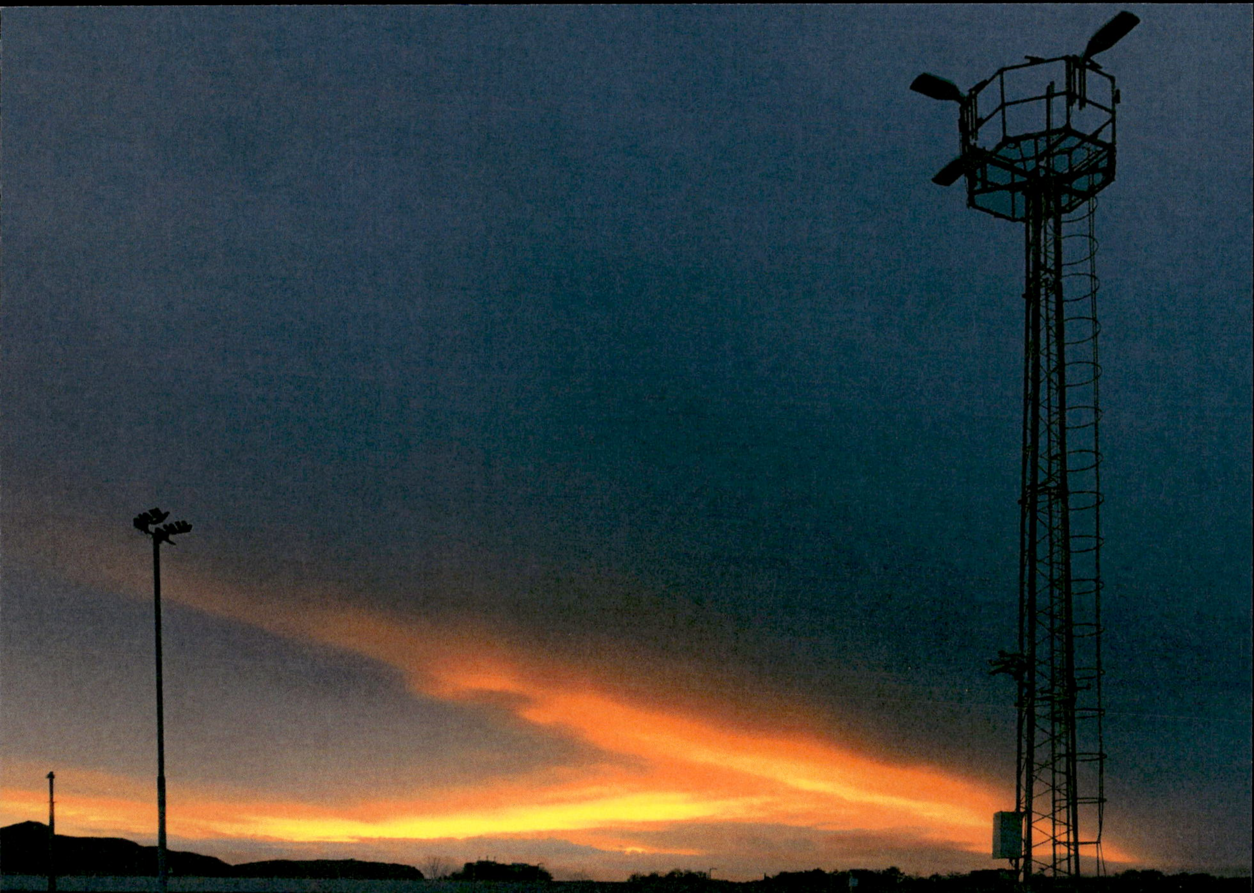

Through This, Or Any Other Valley

Sometimes, when the light is low, and the still air seems to dampen all sound,it is easy to forget you are in the centre of a capital city, surrounded on every side by miles of urban development.

Even on a dreich day Arthur's Seat is infinitely preferable to the rush and noise of the city's traffic. There is a trick that the old mountain plays which is tosomehow slow down time. Time that otherwise seems to career away madly as we pinball our way through the highs and lows of life.

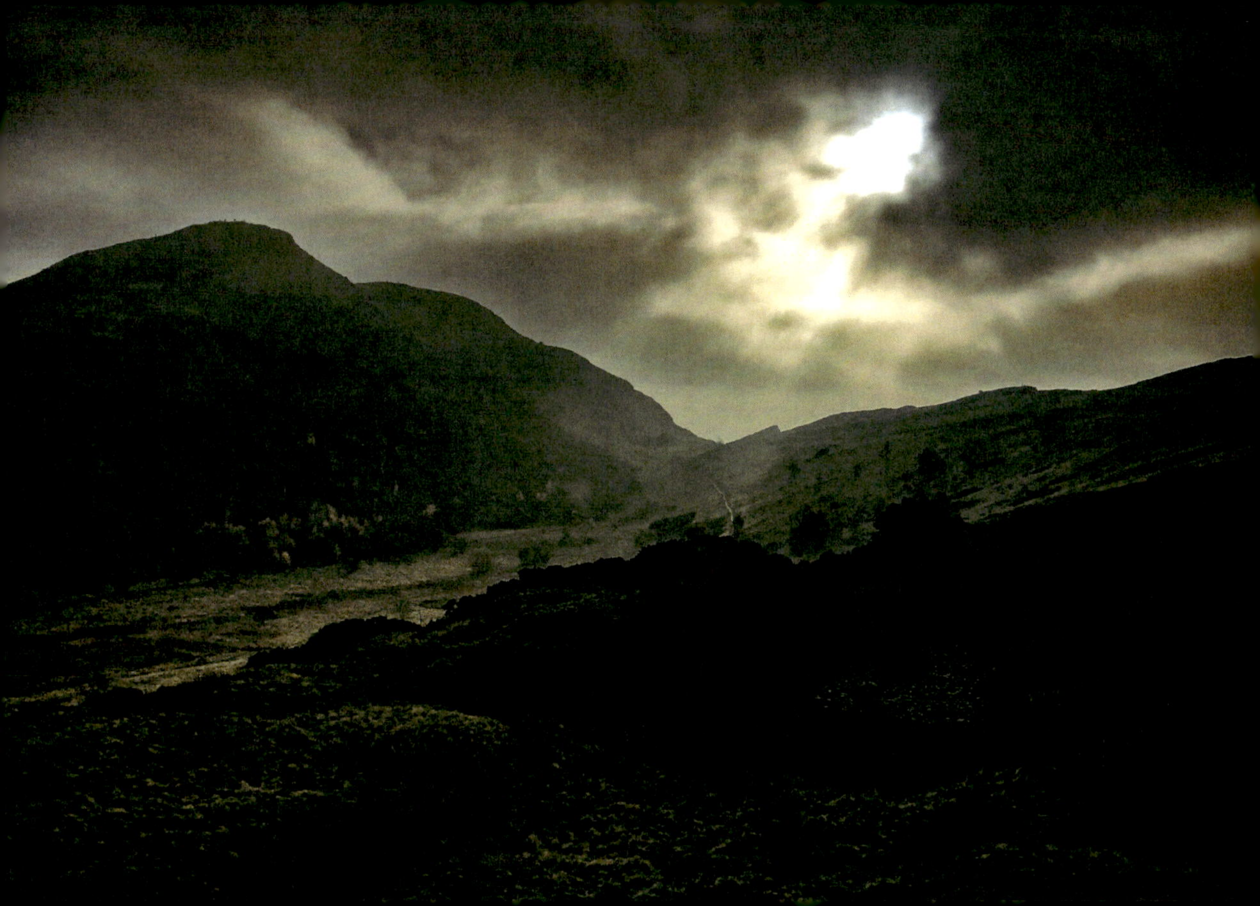

Let Us Turn Our Foreheads To Windward, And Sail On To Better Days

Uncovered by Edinburgh's eternal tram works, here is a reminder that we have lived through other pandemics, other plagues, other hard times.

Some may be left behind, lost along the way, but they are always with us.

May one day we all be buried peacefully beneath the mass-transit schemes of the far-future.

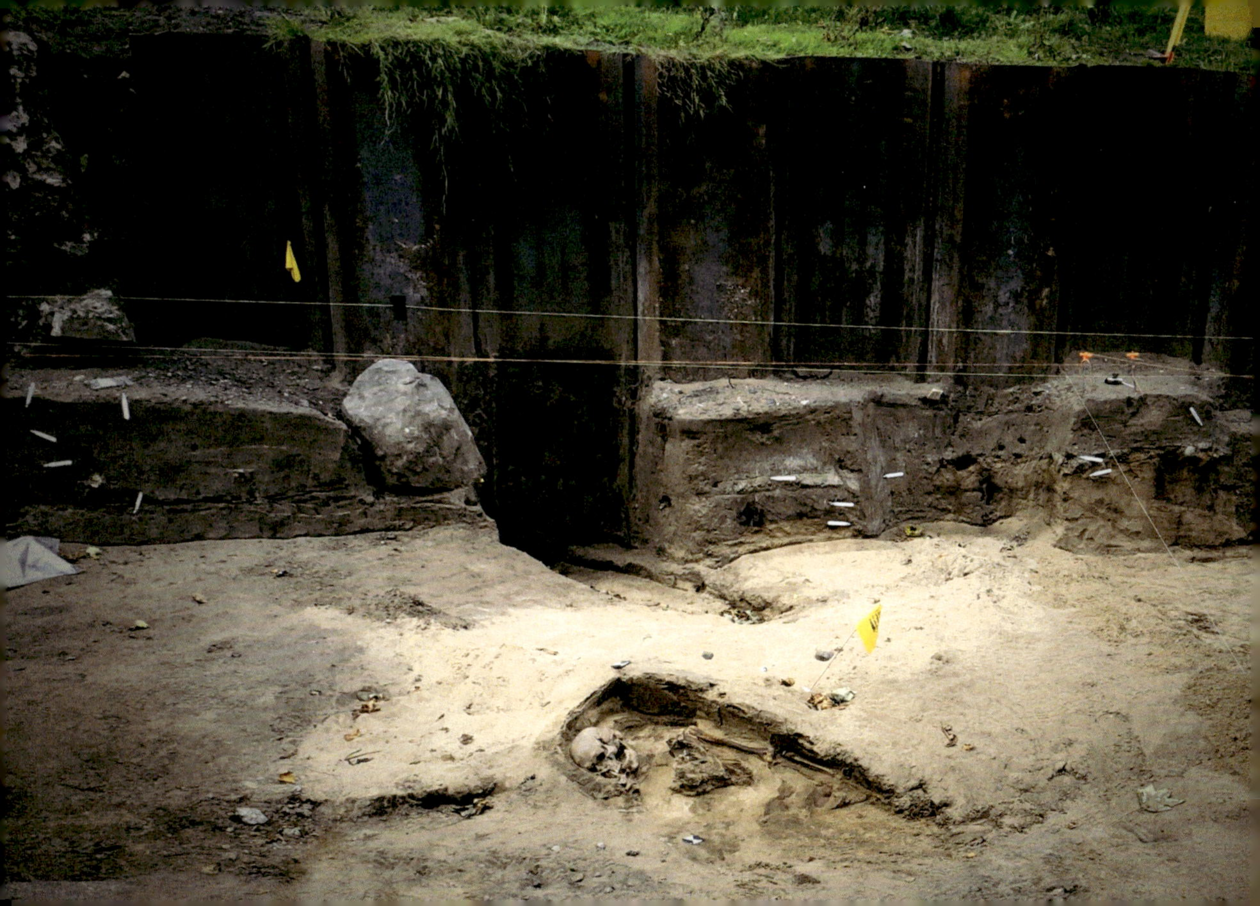

Photography notes

For those that are interested I used several cameras in the making of this book. My trusty Nikon D800 and Nikon D700 cameras were used for the majority of the photographs. Both are thankfully waterproof and have been my constant companions on all my professional photography work for a good few years now.

There are a few photographs taken on my lovely and much-loved Fuji X100. A wonderful camera that makes you want to use it, such is the beauty of its design.

As I subscribe to the ethos that 'the worlds best camera is the one you have in your pocket' then it will come as no surprise to know that I happily used my iPhone 12 for several of the images in the book. Phone camera quality is incredible and getting better all the time.

All the images are digital despite the fact I own four beautiful old film cameras that sit sadly unused on a shelf. Next time!

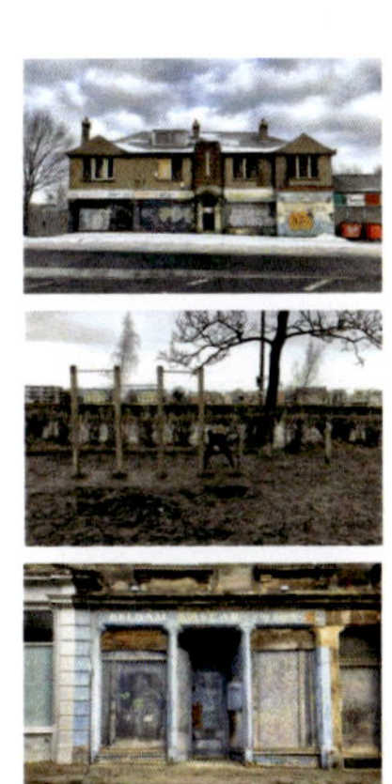

Granton

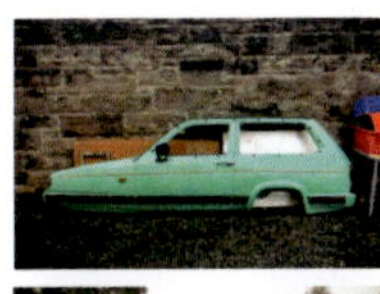

Pilrig

Inverleith Park

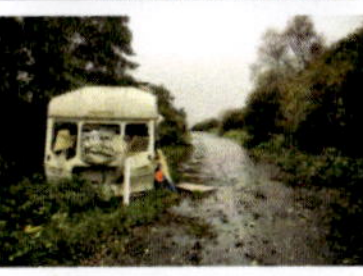

near Liberton

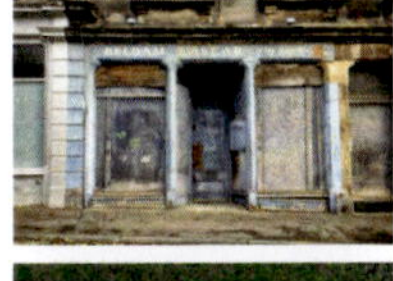

Queen Charlotte Street

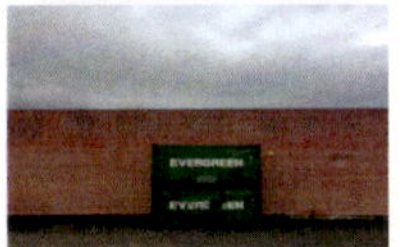

Bankhead

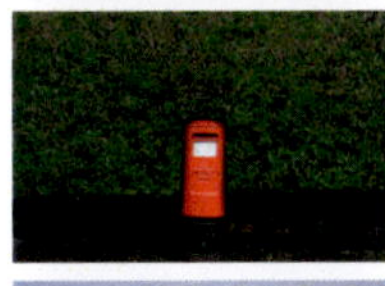

Lochend Road

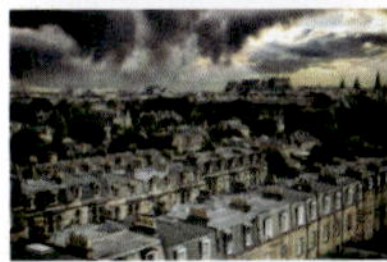

Rooftops, from Merchiston

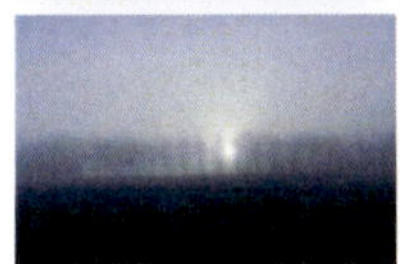

Braid Hills

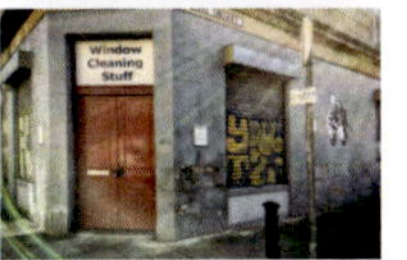

Lorne Street

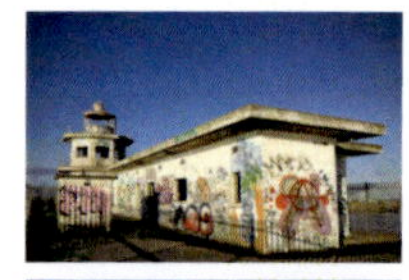

Leith Docks

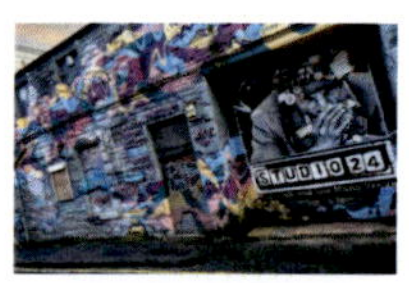

Studio 24, Calton Road

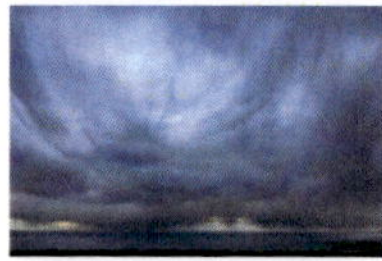

Looking east from Arthur's Seat

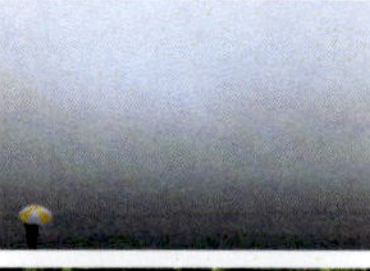

Silverknowes

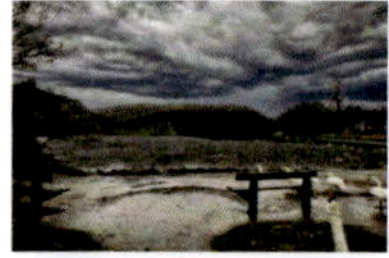

Holyrood Park

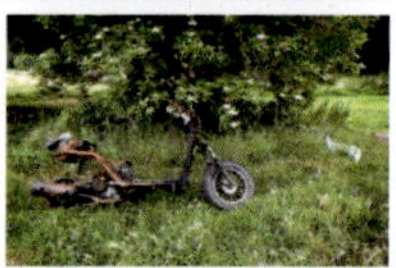

The Hermitage

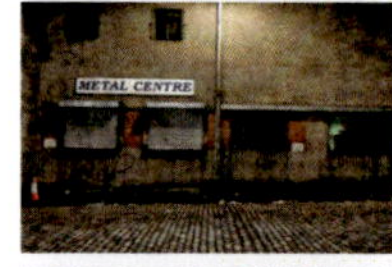

South Fort Street

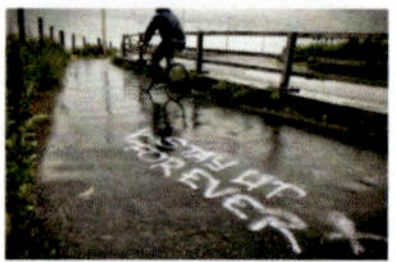

Seafield Road

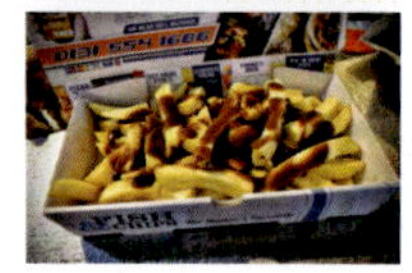

In Chippies throughout
Edinburgh and Hades

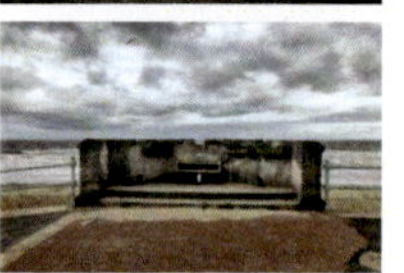

Portobello Beach

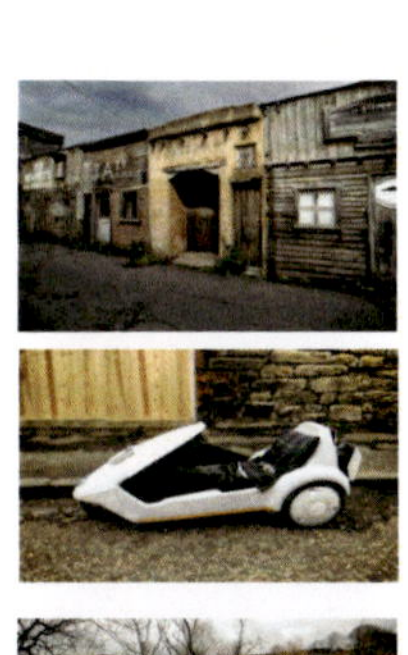

Morningside

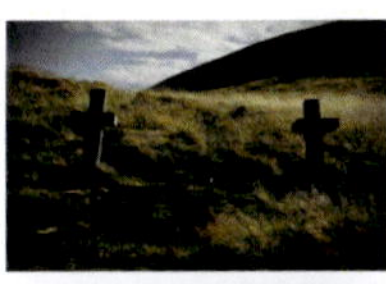

Pentland Hills

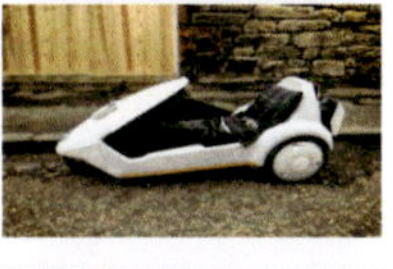

Thirlestane Road

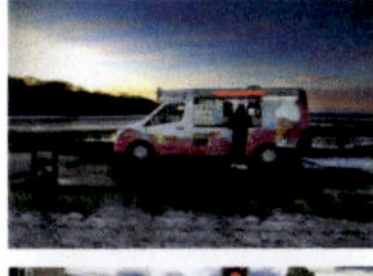

Cramond Village

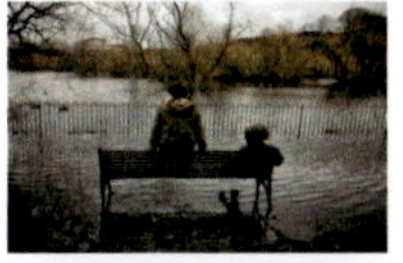

Lochend Park

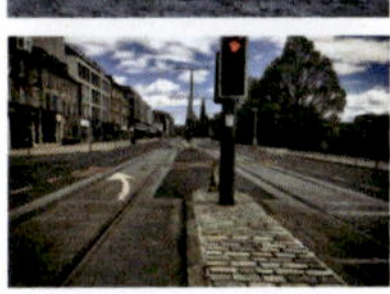

Princes Street

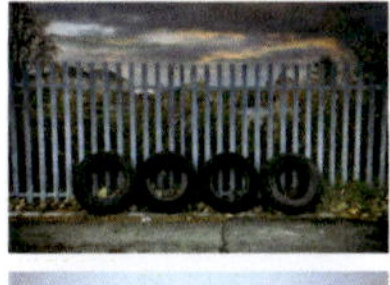

Prospect Bank Road

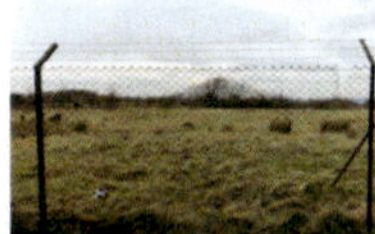

Waterfront Park

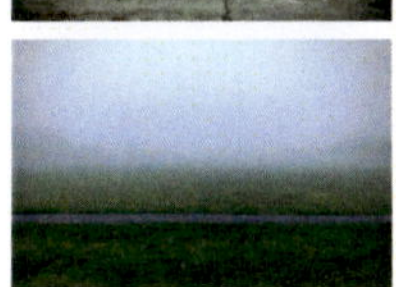

The Meadows

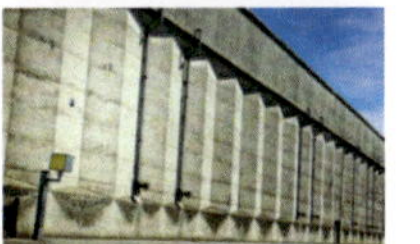

Salamander Street

Colinton Road

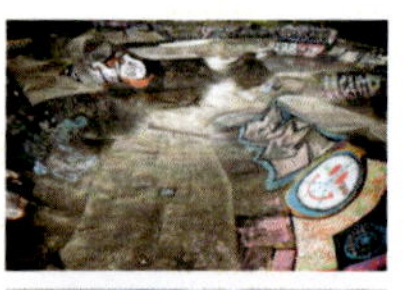

Saughton Park

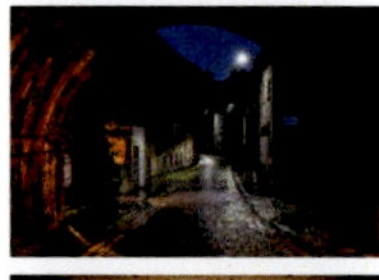

Croft-An-Righ, Holyrood

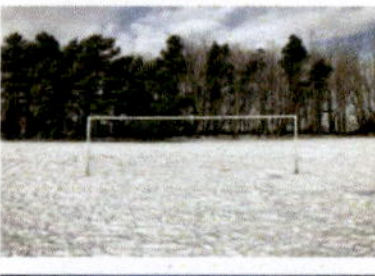

Parsons Green

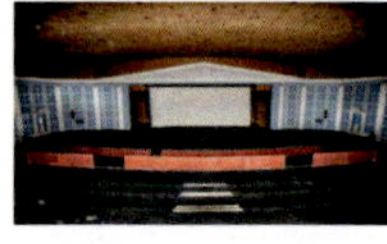

Old Odeon Cinema, Clerk Street

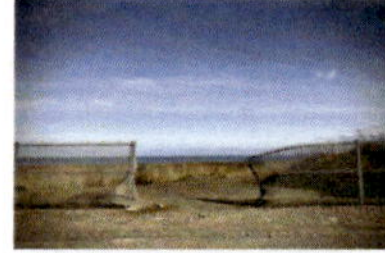

By the sewage works

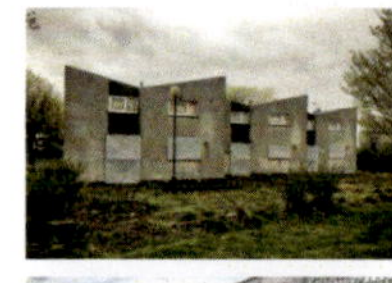

Sighthill

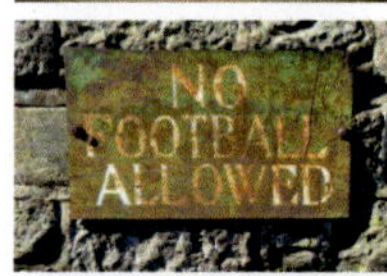

Warriston

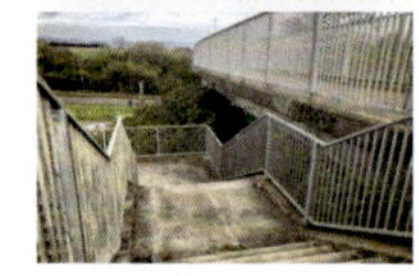

Harry Lauder Road

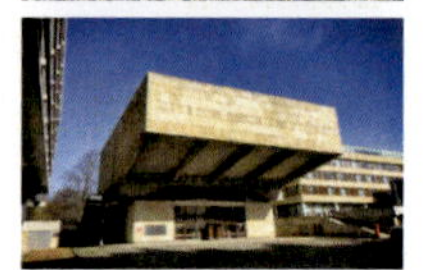

Buccleuch Street

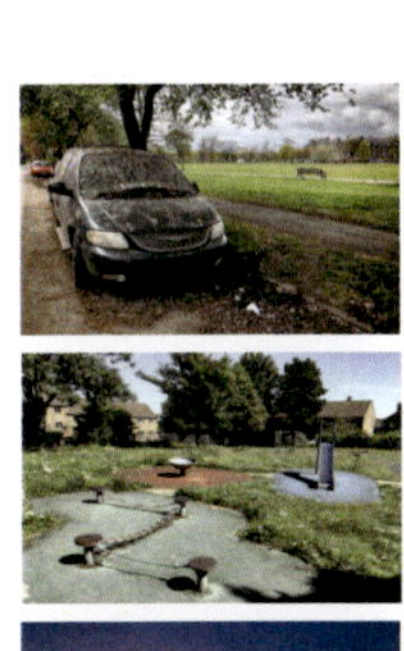

Leith Links

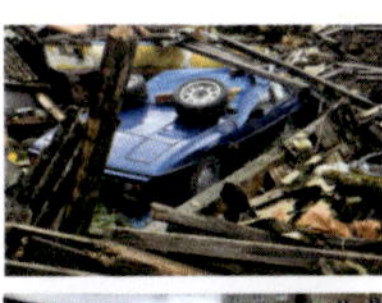

Newcraighall

The Apocalypse Park,
Pirniefield

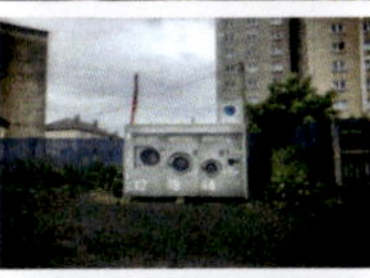

Restalrig Road

West from Calton Hill

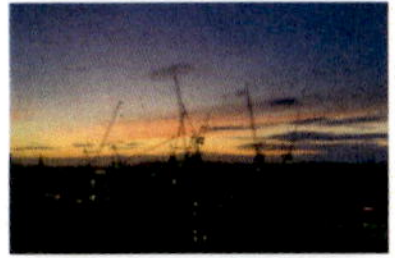

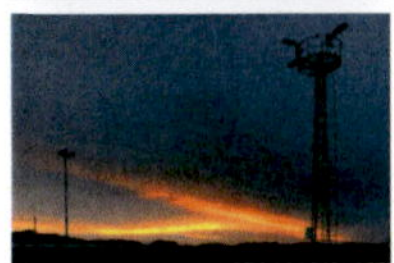

The Dump

Easter Road

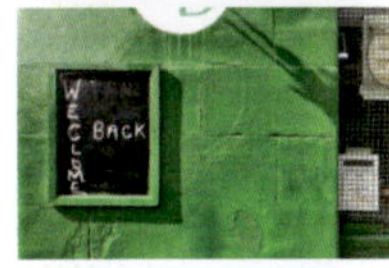

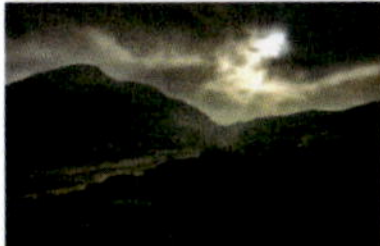

Hunter's Bog, Arthur's Seat

Edinburgh Castle

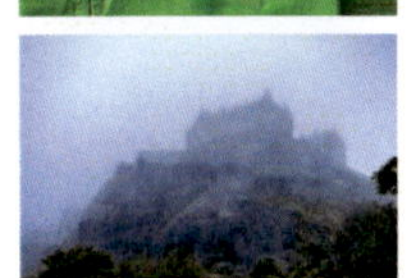

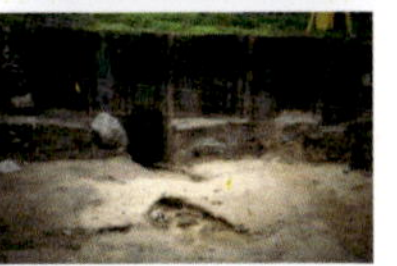

Constitution Street

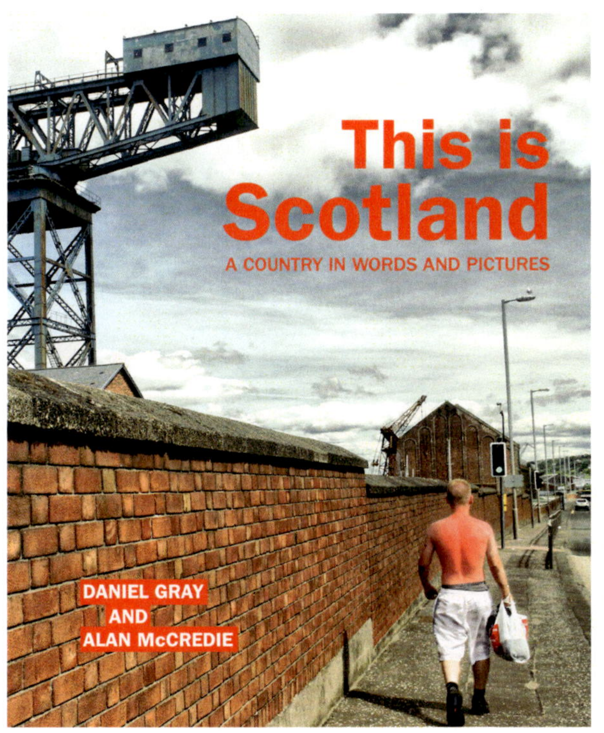

This is Scotland

Daniel Gray and Alan McCredie
ISBN: 978-1-910021-5-90 PBK £6.99

This is Scotland is Daniel Gray's fifth book. His first solo work, *Homage to Caledonia: Scotland and the Spanish Civil War* (Luath), was turned into a two-part television documentary for STV. His second, *Stramash: Tackling Scotland's Towns and Teams* (Luath), received widespread acclaim. An exiled Yorkshireman, he lives in Leith.

Alan McCredie is a freelance photographer who has worked with most major agencies in Scotland and beyond. He has specialised in theatre and television but is perhaps best known for his documentary and travel photography.

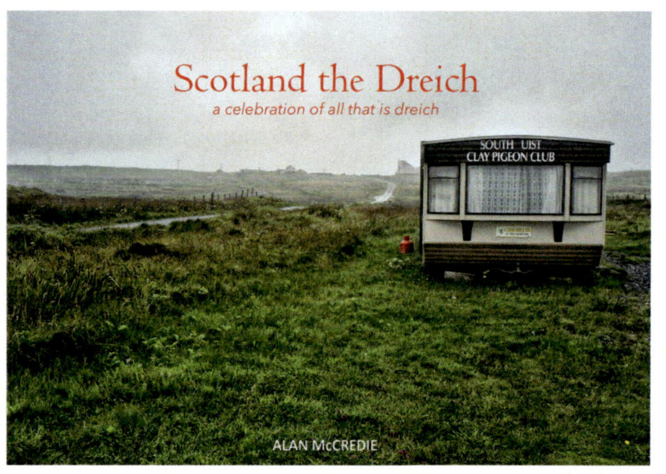

Scotland the Dreich

Alan McCredie
ISBN: 978-1-910745-82-3 PBK £6.99

This book is a celebration of all that is dreich. To my mind the images in this book are uplifting and joyful. There is nothing miserable about dreich. A sunny day has no more right to exist than a dreich one. Here, then, are 50 dreich images, accompanied by 50 equally dreich captions.

Scotland the Braw

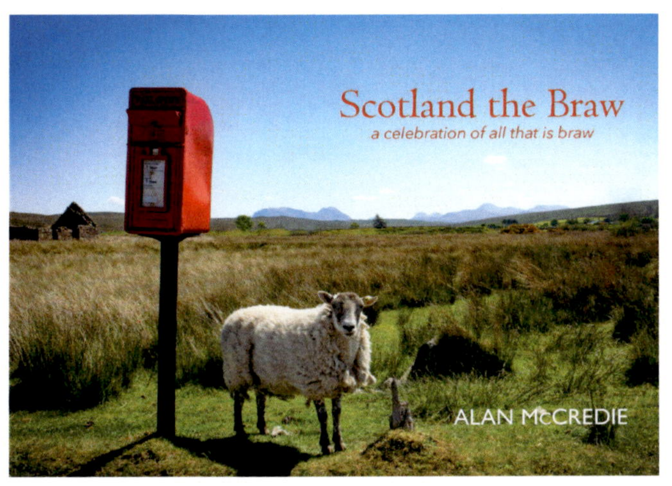

Alan McCredie
ISBN: 978-1-913025-48-9 PBK £6.99

This is a celebration of all that is braw, from the warmth of a Scottish pub to the beauty of the Highland hills, from sunbathing on a dual carriageway to weathering the Beast from the East. Dive into braw Scotland.

Tribes of Glasgow

Stephen Millar & Alan McCredie
ISBN: 978-1912147-85-4 PBK £9.99

Stephen Millar and Alan McCredie took to the streets of Scotland's largest city to depict the multitude of groups, both old and modern, that make up its population.

From cowboys to cosplayers, barras traders to bikers, and gunslingers to goths, forget Humans of New York – these are the Tribes of Glasgow.

From cowboys to cosplayers, barras traders to bikers, and gunslingers to goths, forget Humans of New York – these are the Tribes of Glasgow.

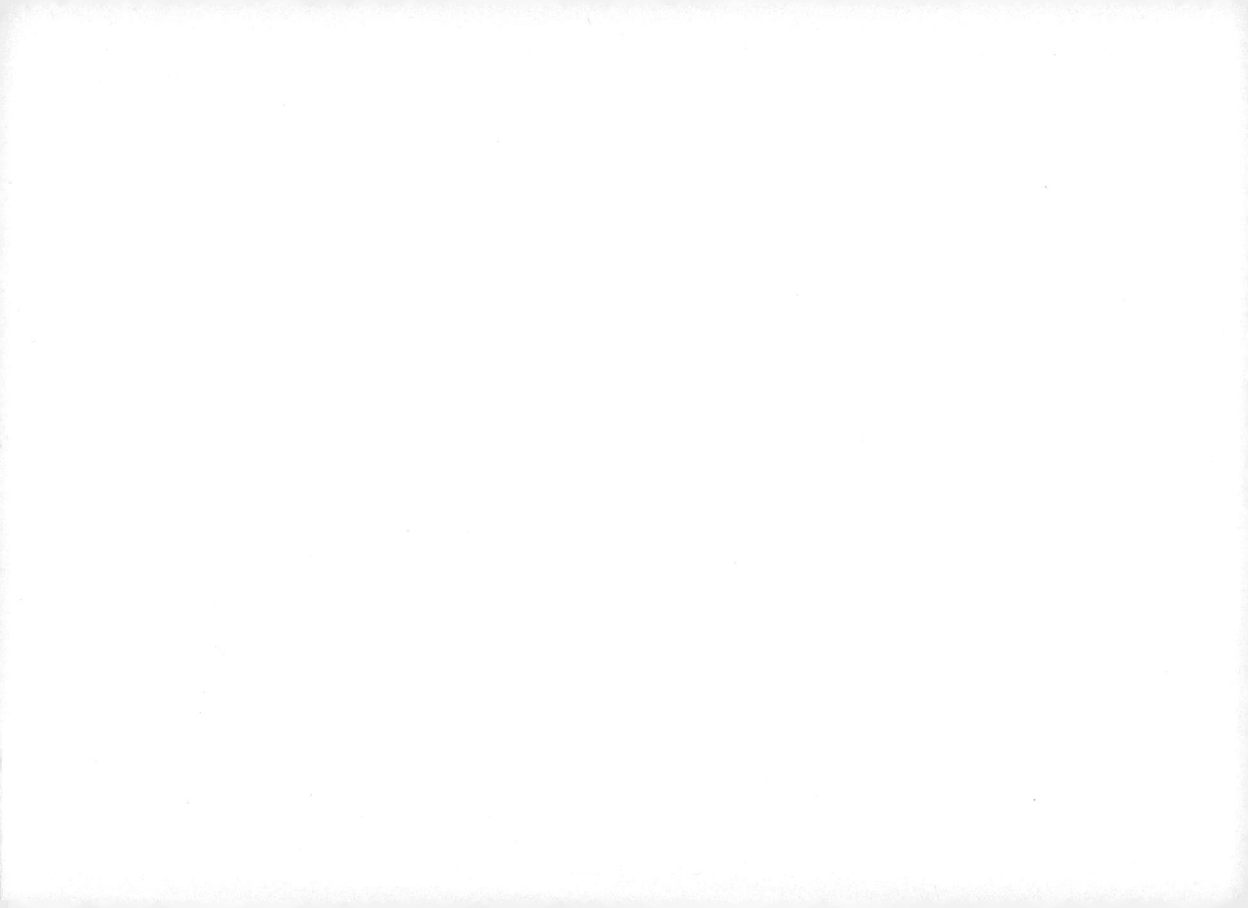

Luath Press Limited

committed to publishing well written books worth reading

LUATH PRESS takes its name from Robert Burns, whose little collie Luath (*Gael.*, swift or nimble) tripped up Jean Armour at a wedding and gave him the chance to speak to the woman who was to be his wife and the abiding love of his life. Burns called one of the 'Twa Dogs' Luath after Cuchullin's hunting dog in Ossian's *Fingal*. Luath Press was established in 1981 in the heart of Burns country, and is now based a few steps up the road from Burns' first lodgings on Edinburgh's Royal Mile. Luath offers you distinctive writing with a hint of unexpected pleasures.

Most bookshops in the UK, the US, Canada, Australia, New Zealand and parts of Europe, either carry our books in stock or can order them for you. To order direct from us, please send a £sterling cheque, postal order, international money order or your credit card details (number, address of cardholder and expiry date) to us at the address below. Please add post and packing as follows: UK – £1.00 per delivery address; overseas surface mail – £2.50 per delivery address; overseas airmail – £3.50 for the first book to each delivery address, plus £1.00 for each additional book by airmail to the same address. If your order is a gift, we will happily enclose your card or message at no extra charge.

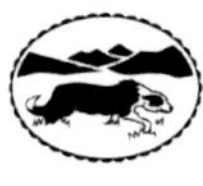

Luath Press Limited
543/2 Castlehill
The Royal Mile
Edinburgh EH1 2ND
Scotland
Telephone: +44 (0)131 225 4326 (24 hours)
Email: sales@luath.co.uk
Website: www.luath.co.uk